DEDICATION

To *Mom and Dad,*
with my love and appreciation.

Sandy

CONTENTS

SCRAP SAVER'S
COUNTRY STITCHERY

·

SANDRA
LOUNSBURY
FOOSE

Library of Congress Catalog Number: 93-083173
Hardcover ISBN: 0-8487-1116-5
Softcover ISBN: 0-8487-1178-5
Manufactured in the United States of America
First Printing 1993

Editor-in-Chief:	Nancy Janice Fitzpatrick
Senior Crafts Editor:	Susan Ramey Wright
Senior Editor, Editorial Services:	Olivia Kindig Wells
Director of Manufacturing:	Jerry Higdon
Art Director:	James Boone

Scrap Saver's Country Stitchery

Editor:	Barbara H. Abrelat
Editorial Assistant:	Patricia Weaver
Designers:	Connie Formby, Eleanor Cameron
Senior Photographer:	John O'Hagan
Photostylist:	Katie Stoddard
Copy Chief:	Mary Jean Haddin
Assistant Copy Editor:	L. Amanda Owens
Copy Assistant:	Leslee Rester Johnson
Production Manager:	Rick Litton
Associate Production Manager:	Theresa L. Beste
Production Assistant:	Marianne Jordan
Assistant Art Director:	Cynthia R. Cooper
Computer Artist:	Carol Loria
Senior Production Designer:	Larry Hunter
Publishing Systems Administrator:	Rick Tucker

COZY DAYS

HOLLY DAYS

INTRODUCTION

Seasons in the country come softly at first. With each passing day, Mother Nature offers her generous gifts of the season, impressing us with her good taste, inspiring us with her creativity, delighting us with her sense of humor. As we watch in wonder, subtle variations in light and color, sound and scent give way to ever more dramatic changes—the first crocus pushing away its winter-leaf blanket, a sky-ful of sunshine and raindrops together at the same moment in time, piles of fragrant apples waiting for a home, lacy snowflakes drifting past crayon-colored trees. For nature's bountiful gifts, we could probably write thank-you notes to fill up every single space on each calendar page throughout the year!

This country scrapbook celebrates the seasons. Projects are arranged in seasonal chapters, but many designs will be comfortably at home in more than one place. You won't need lots of time and money to use these ideas. Almost all the projects have been simplified and streamlined to be very affordable and sometimes even free. Before you get started, however, take a few moments to read the Supplies and Techniques section, beginning on page 154.

Country has different meanings for different folks. For me, it's a make-do mixture of traditions and innovations linking us to people and places in the past, while enhancing our enjoyment of the present moment. Country is a warmhearted look, an open-armed welcome, a feeling of being "at home." But it's not just in "the look," it's also in "the looking," enabling us to see the possibilities in a tattered quilt, a jar of buttons, a ball of twine, and in all the treasures that nature provides.

So as you use this book to create your own gifts of the season, be sure to look outside your window and seek your inspiration from Mother Nature. In city loft and country cottage, fill bowls and baskets, bags and boxes with the fruits and flowers of her handiwork, making your home country at heart!

BREEZY DAYS

Open the windows to welcome springtime's Breezy Days! Every day brings more light, more warmth, and more color into our lives. Much like the season, this chapter is filled with surprises and sentimental celebrations of the heart. A morning of spring-cleaning just might provide some of the materials— scrapsof paper, pastel socks, balls of twine, packing straw, ribbon remnants, and maybe even an egg carton or two!

COUNTRY FRIENDS

◆

These grazing sheep made from balls of twine or yarn bring spring meadows to mind. Tiny scrap-paper birdhouses cheer up a dark corner or hide a secret gift. Turn a lonesome sock into a lovable pastel piggy toy or rattle. And what could welcome spring more than baby birds resting in their own easy-to-make braided nest?

SHEEP TRIO

Materials for three sheep
Pattern on page 36
4"-diameter ball of yarn for large sheep
2½"-diameter ball of cotton twine for medium sheep
1¼"-diameter ball of tatting thread for small sheep
Scraps of neutral-colored art paper or sandpaper
Craft knife
⅛" paper punch
Darning needle
White glue
Compass (optional)
Dried flowers (optional)

Instructions
1. Trace pattern pieces, transferring markings. Cut out. On right side of paper, trace large head and markings. Using craft knife, cut out head. Cut ears, eyes, and "Y" for nose and mouth. Lightly score all fold lines. Repeat for medium head and small head, using paper punch to make eyes on medium head and using needle to make eyes on small head. If optional discs to cover back openings are desired, on remaining paper, use compass to draw circles slightly larger than diameter of each core; cut out. Set aside.
2. To shape each head, make straight folds at nose tab and along head. Make curved folds at top front and back of head. Fold straight across top of each ear and pinch scored ear curves.
3. Slide nose tab into "Y" on wrong side of face and secure with a dot of glue. When dry, trim jaw line on back to match jaw line on front, if necessary. Overlap 1 front side tab over back tab and glue. Repeat for other side. Glue head in place, covering opening in 1 end of yarn ball. Glue dried flowers behind mouth, if desired.
4. To complete large sheep, trace 4 large legs and cut out. Overlap ends ¼" on each and glue to form 4 cylinders. Secure with paper clips until dry. Glue each leg in place. Repeat to make legs for medium and small sheep, overlapping ends ⅛" for small sheep. Insert disc in back opening of each ball, if desired.

BIRDHOUSE GIFT BOX OR ORNAMENT

Materials for one box
Pattern on page 37
6" x 7½" piece of art paper
1 playing card *or* 2⅜" x 3½" piece of sandpaper or corrugated card-board for roof
Craft knife
⅛" paper punch
White glue
Round toothpick or bamboo skewer
6" of string or thread to match paper for ornament
Fine straw for gift box

Instructions
1. Trace pattern, transferring markings. Cut out.
2. From art paper, cut out 1 birdhouse. Transfer pattern markings to right side of house. Use craft knife to lightly score fold lines and to cut out large hole. Use paper punch to make small hole. Reserve punched-out paper dot for end of perch. Fold along all fold lines. Glue side flap to left inside edge of birdhouse front. Clip bottom flap, but do not glue.
3. For roof, score numbered side of playing card widthwise across center and fold in half. (For cardboard or sandpaper roof, score right side widthwise across center and fold in half.) For ornament, use a needle to make a small hole in center of roof fold line. Thread 3 strands of string through hole from wrong side of roof, make a loop, and reinsert through hole; knot ends of string inside roof. Glue ends to inside of roof.
4. Glue top flaps of house to inside of roof. Leave bottom flap open. For perch, cut 1 (⅝" x 1") scrap of art paper and gently pull over blade of scissors to curl. Tightly roll paper around toothpick or skewer. Glue along 1 long edge and hold until dry. Slide paper off and apply small amount of glue to 1 end of perch; insert ⅛" into birdhouse. Glue reserved punched-out dot to end of perch.
5. For ornament, fold and glue bottom flap to inside of birdhouse to close. For gift box, insert a light-weight gift through bottom, add fine straw, and fold flap to close.

LITTLE PIGGY SOCK TOY

Materials for one pig

1 (2½" x 11") woman's stretch sport sock with terry cloth lining

14" (⅛"-wide) of coordinating satin ribbon

9" of round cord elastic for tutu (optional)

18" (1"-wide) of ruffled eyelet lace for tutu (optional)

Thread to match

Embroidery floss: light brown for eyes, slightly darker than sock color for nose

Polyester stuffing

Large jingle bell (optional)

Vanishing fabric marker

Instructions

Note: For safety's sake, every attachment on pig must be double- or triple-stitched with doubled thread. Tug each to check for sturdiness.

1. Cut off 4" cuff portion of sock, as shown in Diagram 1. (Because sock sizes differ, all dimensions are approximate.) Referring to Diagram 1, cut 1 tail and 4 leg pieces.

2. Turn foot portion of sock to terry cloth side. (Terry cloth side will always be considered to be *right* side.) Flatten sock; trim straight across to remove toe seam. Referring to Diagram 1, cut 4¼" section for nose/head/body piece. Set aside. From remainder, cut 2 ear pieces and 1 (1¾"-diameter) circle for nose cover, as indicated in Diagram 1. Set aside.

3. For tail, stretch 2½" strip to 3". Long edges will roll, forming a ¼"-diameter cylinder. Overlap cut edge with finished edge; slipstitch together along long finished edge. Overcast raw edges together at each short end of roll. Beginning 1" away from 1 end, run gathering stitches along length, through 1 layer only; pull thread to gather and curl tail. Tie off. Set aside.

4. Turn nose/head/body piece to wrong side. Measuring ¼" from 1 cut end, mark pig back gathering line (see Diagram 1). Run gathering stitches along this line and pull thread to gather loosely. Insert curled section of tail through opening in gathered body unit, leaving 1" of straight tail outside tube. Pull

Diagram 1: Cutting Sock

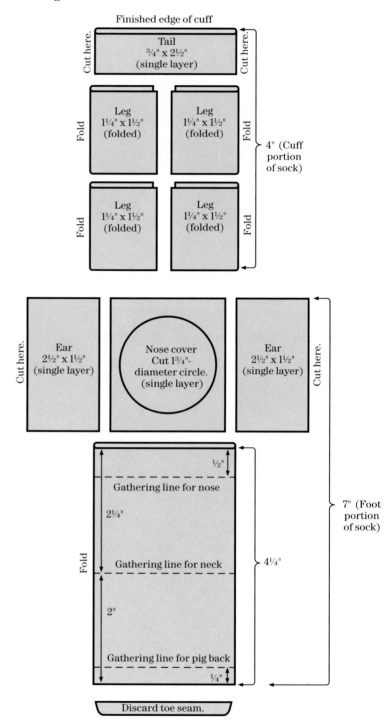

Diagram 2: Making Ears

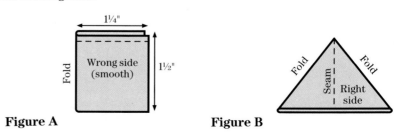

Figure A   Figure B

gathering thread tightly around tail. Wrap loose thread around gathered edge and tail; then stitch by hand back and forth through tail and seam allowance to secure. Tie off.

Turn body right side out. Measuring 2¼" from remaining open end, mark neck gathering line. Then mark nose gathering line ½" from open end.

5. With right sides facing, fold 1 ear piece in half widthwise to measure 1¼" x 1½". Referring to Diagram 2, Figure A, stitch along top edge of ear. Turn right side out and fold to form triangle, as shown in Figure B. Whipstitch open edges closed. Run gathering stitches along whipstitched edge and pull to gather to measure 2". Tie off. Repeat to make remaining ear. With center seams facing front of pig, position ears 1" apart on marked neckline and whipstitch.

6. Stuff body section firmly. If making rattle, bury jingle bell deep in stuffing. Run gathering stitches along neckline, catching ears in stitching. Put thumb inside neckline and pull gathering threads tightly to fit around thumb. Tie off.

7. Stuff head firmly. Run gathering stitches along nose line. With nose seam allowance to outside of body unit, pull gathering thread very tightly. Tie off.

Turn edge of nose cover under ¼" and hem. Run gathering stitches along hemmed edge and pull gently to form a cup shape. Place cover over nose seam allowance and pull thread to fit. Slipstitch securely in place. Flatten nose and mold head to form a ball. To make pig look chubby, slipstitch head to body, shortening neck area. Pull ears forward and curl them slightly.

8. Unfold 1 leg piece, turn under ¼"

along 1 long cut edge, and hem. With right sides facing, refold widthwise. Machine-stitch together cut edges opposite fold. Run gathering stitches ¼" from cut edge opposite hem. Pull gathering thread tightly and tie off. Turn leg right side out and stuff firmly. Repeat for remaining legs. Referring to photo for placement, securely slipstitch each leg to body.

9. Using 2 strands of light brown embroidery floss, make French knots for eyes. Using 2 strands of floss darker than sock, satin-stitch 2 (¼") circles on nose. Tie ribbon in bow around neck and tack securely.

For optional tutu, thread cord elastic through casing formed by lace binding. Tie ends of elastic together. Fold raw edges of lace under; overlap folded edges and slipstitch together. Place tutu on pig, distributing ruffle evenly, and tack securely.

BABY BIRDS IN A BRAIDED NEST

Materials for one nest
3 (1⅞" x 44") strips of fabric
3¾ yards (⅜") of cotton filler cord
Thread to match
Bodkin or large safety pin
Masking tape
Large sturdy needle
Rubber bands

Instructions
1. With right sides facing and raw edges aligned, fold 1 fabric strip in half lengthwise. Stitch long edges together. Using bodkin or safety pin, turn strip right side out. Repeat with remaining fabric strips.

2. Measure filler cord into 3 equal lengths and mark by wrapping masking tape around cord at each division. Cut cord through center of tape at each section. Using bodkin or safety pin, pull 1 length of cord through 1 fabric tube. Trim cord at each end, ¾" shorter than tube; tack cord ends to tube. Repeat with remaining fabric tubes and filler cord.

3. To make braid, align 3 tubes at 1 end and stitch together. Tape or pin unit to work surface. Roll up each tube and secure each rolled tube with rubber band. Make flat braid, unrolling tubes as needed and securing braid with a rubber band at end.

4. Beginning at stitched end, coil and stack braid to form nest, slipstitching long edges together as you work. At end of braid, remove rubber band, tuck raw ends inside fabric tubes, and slipstitch to outside of nest.

Materials for one bird
Pattern on page 37
7¼" x 13¼" piece of print fabric
1¼" x 1¾" scrap of tan fabric for beak
14" (1/16"-wide) of coordinating satin ribbon
Thread to match
Polyester stuffing
Black embroidery floss
Vanishing fabric marker

Instructions
1. Trace pattern pieces, transferring markings. Cut out.

2. With right sides facing, fold print fabric in half lengthwise. Place pattern pieces on fabric ½" apart and trace 1 body back, 1 body front, 2 wings, and 2 head pieces, transferring markings. *Do not cut out yet.* Pin layers of fabric together within each traced shape.

3. Machine-stitch along angled center seam of body back, center seams of body front, and each head piece. Machine-stitch completely around each wing. Cut out all pieces, adding ¼" seam allowances.

On *stitched* seams, trim seam allowances to ⅛" and clip curves. Staystitch seam lines along open neck edges of head and body. Referring to pattern, make ¾"-long slit through 1 layer only on each wing. Turn wings right side out and slipstitch openings closed.

4. With right sides facing and seams aligned at top, pin 2 head units together. Machine-stitch, leaving open at neck. Trim stitched seam allowance to ⅛", clip curves, and turn. On open neck, clip seam allowance to staystitching; tuck inside head and baste.

With right sides facing and seams aligned at bottom, pin body front and back units together. Machine-stitch, leaving open at neck. Trim stitched seam allowance to ⅛", clip curves, and turn.

*W*elcome spring to any room with a cheerful braided fabric nest and trio of baby blue birds.

5. Stuff head and body firmly. Place head on body, aligning seams. Slipstitch units together. Using 1 strand of floss, satin-stitch eyes.

6. On wrong side of tan fabric, trace 1 beak and cut out, adding ¼" seam allowance. Clip curve. Turn curved edge under ¼" and baste.

With right sides facing, fold beak in half; slipstitch straight edges together to make a cone. Turn right side out and stuff lightly. With seam at bottom of beak aligned with center head seam, slipstitch beak securely to head below eyes.

7. Referring to photo for placement and with slit sides toward body, pin wings to bird. Slipstitch curved edge of wings to body. Tie ribbon in bow around neck and position bow at side of head just above wing.

HEARTS GALORE

◆

This heart-shaped pillow in rich jewel-like colors is a gift that will be enjoyed any time of the year. Add a loving touch to your family's kitchen with a heart pot holder. Recycle paper and cardboard to make keepsake paper hearts. And you can make easy ornaments from scraps of ribbon and lace.

QUILT LOVER'S PILLOW

Materials for one pillow
Pattern on page 38
18" x 28" piece of blue/green/mauve floral print fabric
4" square of blue fabric
6" square of mauve fabric
7½" square of green fabric
Thread: green, mauve
15" square of thin quilt batting
Polyester stuffing
48½" (½"-wide) of green double-fold bias tape
White drawing pencil

Instructions
   1. Trace pattern pieces, transferring markings. Cut out.
   2. For pillow back, cut 2 (9¼" x 18") pieces from print fabric. With right sides facing and raw edges aligned, pin pieces together along 1 long edge. Machine-stitch along pinned edge, leaving a 4" opening in center of seam. Press seam open. Set aside.
   3. For pillow front, place pattern pieces on wrong side of fabrics, ½" apart. Trace and cut pieces from fabrics as indicated on pattern, adding ¼" seam allowances.
   4. Referring to Diagram 1, assemble patchwork block. Press seams open. Referring to Diagram 2, assemble heart to complete pillow front. Press seams open.
   5. Stack back (right side down); batting; and patchwork heart (right side up), centering patchwork heart on center seam of pillow back. Pin layers together. Machine-stitch completely around heart through all layers, ¼" from raw edge. Repeat, stitching ¹⁄₁₆" from raw edge.
   6. Trim excess back and batting ⅛" outside of raw edge of pillow front. Bind edges with bias tape. Stuff pillow through opening in back. Slipstitch opening closed.

PATCHWORK POT HOLDER

Materials for one pot holder
Pattern on page 39
5½" x 13" piece of blue/green/mauve floral print fabric
2½" square of blue fabric
10" square of fabric for backing
5" square of mauve fabric
6" square of green fabric
Thread: mauve, green
40" (½"-wide) of green double-fold bias tape
10" square of extra-thick quilt batting
White drawing pencil

Instructions
   1. Trace pattern pieces, transferring markings. Cut out.
   2. Referring to Steps 3–6 of Quilt Lover's Pillow, at left, complete pot holder, using 10" square of fabric for backing, omitting opening and stuffing, and reserving excess bias tape.
   3. For hanger, cut 6½" length from remaining bias tape. Turn cut ends under and stitch. Fold tape to form loop and tack ends to back of heart at center top.

BIG-HEARTED POT HOLDER

Materials
10" square of print fabric for front
10" square of print fabric for backing
Thread to match
10" square of extra-thick quilt batting
40" (½"-wide) of double-fold bias tape

Instructions
   1. For heart pattern, draw a 4⅞" square. Trace pot holder pattern piece F, page 39, on 2 adjacent sides of square.
   2. Center pattern on right side of 1 print fabric square and trace heart. *Do not cut out yet.*
   3. Stack backing (right side down); batting; and marked print fabric square (right side up). Pin and baste layers together. Machine-stitch through all layers along outline. Cut out, adding ⅜" seam allowance. Bind edges with bias tape, reserving excess tape.
   4. Referring to Step 3 of Patchwork Pot Holder, above, add hanger.

The Quilt Lover's Pillow (top), Big-Hearted Pot Holder (center), and Patchwork Pot Holder (bottom) come by their country charm naturally, with Amish-inspired jewel-tone fabrics and a traditional quilt pattern.

**Diagram 1:
Assembling Patchwork Block**

Row 1   C   B D B   C

Row 2   B D B   A   B D B

Row 3   C   B B D   C

**Diagram 2:
Assembling Heart**

F

C B D B C
B B
E D A D
B B
C B D B C

F

A   E

17

SMALL PAPER HEART ORNAMENT

Materials for one heart

Pattern on page 39
2 (3") squares of corrugated light
    bulb package
Craft knife
White glue
12" (¹⁄₁₆"-wide) of satin ribbon
Red fine-point marker (optional)

Instructions

1. Trace small heart pattern and cut out. On smooth side of corrugated paper pieces, trace 2 hearts and cut out.

2. Cut 5" length of ribbon and fold in half to form a loop. On back of 1 heart, glue ends of loop to center top. Apply glue to back of remaining heart. Gently press 2 hearts together.

If desired, draw lines between corrugated ridges with red marker.

3. Apply a small amount of glue around edge of heart. Starting at center top, glue remaining ribbon around heart to cover edges.

LARGE PAPER HEART ORNAMENT

Materials for one heart

Pattern on page 39
2 (4") squares of black-and-white
    notebook cover cardboard
3" square of opaque white paper
Craft knife
Black fine-point marker
White glue
6" (¹⁄₈"-wide) of grosgrain ribbon
11½" (¹⁄₄"-wide) of black double-fold
    bias tape

Instructions

1. Trace notebook label and large heart pattern and cut out. Cut 1 heart from each notebook cover cardboard square. On white paper, trace 1 label pattern, transferring markings. With marker, draw borders and lines. Cut out label and glue in center of 1 cardboard heart.

2. Fold ribbon in half to form a loop. Glue ends of loop to back of labeled heart at center top. Apply glue to 1 side of remaining cardboard heart and press to back of other heart.

3. Starting at center top, glue bias tape to front and back of heart, covering edges.

RUFFLED PAPER HEART ORNAMENT

Materials for one heart

Pattern on page 39
2 (3") squares of file folder
10"-wide lightweight paper bag with
    serrated top edge
Craft knife
Rubber cement
6" (¹⁄₁₆"-wide) of satin ribbon or string
Small piece of cellulose sponge
    (optional)
Food coloring (optional)

Instructions

1. Trace small heart pattern and cut out. Cut 1 heart from each folder piece. Cut 2 (1" x 10") strips from serrated edge of paper bag. From remainder of bag, cut 2 (3") squares.

For optional spongeware-look, dip sponge in undiluted food coloring. Squeeze sponge, blot on paper towel to remove excess coloring, and lightly dab coloring on paper squares.

2. Apply thin layer of rubber cement to back of 1 paper square and to 1 side of 1 folder heart. Let dry. Turn heart over and apply glue around outside ½" edge. Let dry. With fully cemented sides facing, center heart on square and press

18

pieces together. Trim paper within ¼" of heart shape. Clip paper to heart edge at ⅛" intervals. Fold paper over edge and press to back of heart. Repeat with other heart.

3. Apply thin layer of cement to back of each heart and ½" along long straight cut edge of each serrated paper strip. Let dry. Starting at center top of 1 heart and ending at point, press cemented edge of 1 paper strip to back of heart, pinching and pleating strip as you work. Repeat with remaining strip to add paper ruffle to other half of heart. If desired, touch sponge dipped in food coloring to serrated edges of ruffle.

4. Fold ribbon or string in half to form a loop. Cement ends of loop to back of 1 ruffled heart at center top. Apply another thin layer of cement to back of ruffled hearts. When dry, gently press 2 hearts together.

RUFFLED RIBBON HEART

Materials for one heart
27" (1½"-wide) of red grosgrain ribbon
6" (⅛"-wide) of red grosgrain ribbon
Thread to match
1 (12"-long) chenille stem

Instructions
1. On each cut end of 1½"-wide ribbon, turn under ⅛" and slipstitch. To make casing, turn 1 long edge under ⅜" and machine-stitch.

2. Bend 1 end of chenille stem ½", making a hook. Thread straight end of stem through ribbon casing, gathering ribbon and catching hook at beginning of casing. Pull straight end of stem outside casing and trim off 4½". Bend cut end ½" and interlock with other hook, forming ribbon into a ring. Distribute gathers, covering stem. Slipstitch hemmed ends of ribbon together, concealing cut edges.

3. Fold narrow ribbon in half to form a loop. Tack ends of loop to gathered ribbon where hemmed ends are joined. Bend stem into heart shape.

LACY HEART ORNAMENT

Materials for one heart
10" (¾"-wide) of crocheted lace
6" (⅛"-wide) of satin ribbon
Thread to match
1 (2½"-wide) heart-shaped cookie cutter
Plastic sandwich bag
Spray starch
Rubber band

Instructions
1. Wrap lace around cookie cutter to check length and trim excess lace, if necessary. Whipstitch cut ends of lace together to form a ring. On protected surface, saturate lace with spray starch.

2. Place cookie cutter in bag, wrapping plastic around edges of cookie cutter. With seam at top, slide wet lace smoothly over bag-covered cookie cutter. To secure, stretch rubber band over lace from crevice at top of heart to tip.

When dry, spray lace again with starch, repeating as necessary to stiffen.

3. When thoroughly dry, remove lace from cookie cutter. Fold ribbon in half to form a loop and tack ends of loop to heart at seam. Secure heart shape by tacking folds at crevice and at tip.

COUNTRY ACCENT

Whether your celebration is a cozy dinner for two, dessert with drop-in friends, or a pretend tea party for the little ones, surprising touches make it an occasion to remember. In just minutes, dress up plain tea bags with heart-shaped stickers from your stationery store or card shop.

WELCOME BABY!

◆

A baby's birth is a joyous reminder of Mother Nature's gift of new life in the spring. Welcome a newcomer with a soft sacque set, made quickly and inexpensively with pastel bandannas and flannel. Or use a strip of eyelet edging to fashion an easy cap with ribbon ties.

Make the most of a stained or damaged cutwork doily by using the unspoiled portion to make a bib. And bows filled with potpourri can be hung on hangers or tucked in drawers to scent baby's layette.

BANDANNA BABY SACQUE AND CAP SET

Materials for one set
Pattern on pages 40–41
4 bandannas with 3½"-wide border and no center medallion
½ yard of flannel for lining
33" (⅝"-wide) of gathered lace
52" of corded piping
24" (⅜"-wide) of double-face satin ribbon (for optional sacque ties)
32" (⅜"-wide) of double-face satin ribbon (for cap)
Thread to match
Vanishing fabric marker
Zipper foot for sewing machine
Small safety pin

Instructions for sacque
1. Trace pattern pieces, adding sleeve extension as indicated. Cut out.
2. On wrong side of 1 bandanna, align sacque front pattern with corner and trace 1. (Always leave ¼" between edge of bandanna border and edge of each pattern for best look.) Adding ¼" seam allowance, cut out. On wrong side of another bandanna, reverse pattern and repeat to cut other front. Set aside scraps.

On wrong side of third bandanna, with border along bottom edge of pattern and not extending into the arm area, trace 1 back. Adding ¼" seam allowance, cut out. Reverse pattern and repeat to cut other back from remaining bandanna. Set aside scraps.

From flannel, cut 1 front for lining, adding ¼" seam allowance; reverse pattern and cut other lining front. Set aside. Fold remaining flannel in half; align center of back pattern with fold, as indicated on pattern. Trace 1 back. Cut out, adding ¼" seam allowance. Set aside scraps for cap lining.

3. With right sides facing and raw edges aligned, stitch bandanna backs together. (Press all seams open as you work.) With right sides facing and raw edges aligned, stitch 1 front to back at shoulder. Repeat with remaining bandanna front.

Measure and cut 2 (8½") pieces of gathered lace for sleeves. With right sides facing and bound edge of lace aligned with raw edge of sleeve opening, stitch 1 lace piece to 1 sleeve. Fold bound edge of lace and seam allowance to wrong side of sleeve opening and baste. Repeat with remaining sleeve.

With right sides facing and raw edges aligned, stitch 1 side/underarm seam. Stitch seam again to reinforce. Clip curve. Repeat with remaining side.

Trim seam allowance of piping to ¼". Starting at bottom edge of sacque back and with right sides facing, align raw edge of piping with raw edge of sacque. Baste continuous piece of piping around entire sacque. Clip seam allowance of piping at curves. Using zipper foot, machine-stitch piping to sacque along basting line.

4. For lining, stitch 1 front flannel piece to back flannel piece at shoulder.

Repeat with remaining front. To hem sleeves, fold edges under ¼" and baste.

5. With right sides facing, raw edges aligned, and lining sleeves inserted into sacque sleeves, pin sacque and lining together. Beginning on bottom edge of back, stitch together in 1 continuous seam, leaving a 4" opening for turning. (Do not stitch sleeves.) Clip all curved seam allowances and turn. Slipstitch opening closed.

Slipstitch hemmed edge of each lining sleeve to sacque sleeves. Tack lining to sacque at each shoulder and underarm.

If desired, cut 24"-long satin ribbon in half. Turn under ¼" on 1 cut end of each piece; baste. Tack 1 basted end of ribbon to each side of sacque neck opening to make ties.

SHAMROCK PATCHWORK

◆

Start the greening of spring with bright polka-dot patchwork. Use the basic shamrock square to make any of the following projects—pot holder, apron, or small pillow.

SHAMROCK PATCHWORK SQUARE

Materials for one square
Pattern on page 42
4" x 11½" piece of green or green/white dot fabric
4" x 11½" piece of white or white/green dot fabric
Thread to match
Green embroidery floss (for hand-embroidered stem) or 4" square of tear-away stabilizer (for machine-embroidered stem)
Vanishing fabric marker

Instructions
1. Trace pattern pieces A, B, and C, transferring markings. Cut out.
2. From green fabric, cut 3 As. From white fabric, cut 3 Bs and 1 C. On wrong side of all pieces, transfer markings. On right side of C, mark line for stem. On each B, clip curve almost to seam line at ¼" intervals.
3. With right sides of 1 A and 1 B facing, match large dots, align raw edges, and pin together. Machine-stitch, removing pins as you sew. Clip seam allowance again; press seam toward green. Repeat with remaining A/B units.
4. Refer to Diagram 1, Figure A, to assemble shamrock square.
Stem may be embroidered by hand or machine. For hand embroidery, work chainstitch with 3 strands of floss. For machine-embroidered stem, baste stabilizer behind C and machine-satin-stitch on traced line. Tear away stabilizer.

SHAMROCK POT HOLDER

Materials
1 completed shamrock square
7½" square of fabric for backing
34" (½"-wide) of green double-fold bias tape or 34" (1½"-wide) bias strip of green-and-white stripe fabric
Thread to match
2 (7½") squares of quilt batting
¾" white plastic ring

Instructions
1. Center and baste 1 batting square to wrong side of shamrock square. If desired, outline-quilt by hand or machine ¼" inside edges of shamrock. Stack backing (right side down); second batting square; and patchwork square (right side up). Machine-stitch around square ¼" from edges. Repeat, stitching ¹⁄₁₆" from edges. Trim backing and batting ⅛" larger than shamrock square.
2. For binding, use bias tape or turn each long edge of stripe fabric strip under ¼" and press.
Stitch binding to edges, mitering corners. Tack plastic ring to corner corresponding to middle leaf of shamrock.

Diagram 1: Shamrock Square

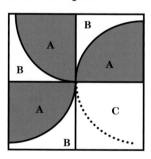

Figure A

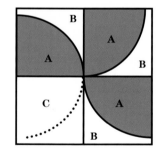

Figure B

SHAMROCK POCKET APRON

Materials
2 completed shamrock squares (1 reversed, as shown in Diagram 1, Figure B)
18" x 44" piece of green check fabric for apron
2 (6½") squares of white fabric for pocket backing
2 (2" x 36") pieces of green/white dot fabric for ties
Thread to match

Instructions
1. Referring to Diagram 2, measure and mark each pocket placement and center point of apron. Turn 1 long edge under ¼" and then ¾"; machine-stitch hem. Along opposite edge, run rows of gathering stitches ¼" and ⅛" from edge. Pull to gather slightly. Set aside.
2. For ties, with right sides facing and raw edges aligned, machine-stitch strips together along 1 short edge. Press seam open. On wrong side of tie strip, measure 11" on each side of center seam and mark with dots. With right sides facing and raw edges aligned, match center seam of tie strip to center dot on gathered

Diagram 2: Making Apron

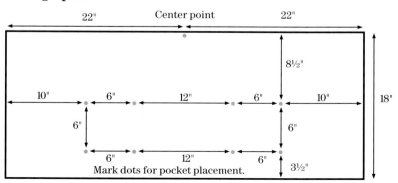

Mark dots for pocket placement.

edge of apron and pin. Distribute gathers to fit within marked dots; pin. Machine-stitch between dots.

With right sides facing, fold tie strip in half lengthwise. Pin and stitch short and long edges together, leaving open along apron edge. Trim corners, turn right side out, and press. Turn open edge under ¼" and press. Machine-stitch. Topstitch waistband and ties.

3. With right sides facing and raw edges aligned, pin 1 shamrock square to 1 white backing square. Machine-stitch ¼" from edges, leaving 3" opening at bottom. Trim corners; turn. Fold raw edges under; press. Topstitch ¼" around inside edges of leaves. Repeat for other pocket. Align pockets with placement marks on apron and pin. Slipstitch sides and bottom of each pocket to apron.

SHAMROCK PILLOW

Materials
Pattern on page 43
1 completed shamrock square
6½" x 15" piece of green-and-white stripe fabric
10" square of fabric for back
33" of green corded piping
Thread to match
Polyester stuffing
12" square of thin quilt batting
Zipper foot for sewing machine

Instructions
1. Trace pattern piece D, transferring markings. Cut out.
2. From stripe fabric, cut 4 Ds, transferring markings. With right side up, center shamrock square on point on batting square and pin.

With right sides facing and raw edges aligned, pin 1 D to 1 side of shamrock square. Stitch between large dots. Press seam allowance toward D. Repeat to join remaining Ds.

Baste edges to batting. If desired, outline-quilt by hand or machine ¼" inside shamrock leaves. Trim excess batting to match size of pillow front.

3. Trim piping seam allowance to ¼". With right sides facing and raw edges aligned, pin piping to pillow front, tapering at start and end. Using zipper foot, machine-stitch piping to pillow front. Clip curves.

4. With right sides facing and raw edges aligned, center pillow front on back; pin. Stitch together along stitching line of piping, leaving 3" opening; trim excess. Clip curves; turn. Stuff pillow firmly. Slipstitch opening closed.

HAPPY EASTER!

◆

All dressed up in jelly bean colors, the Egg Bunny welcomes this springtime holiday. Make single four-bunny units or tape several units together to make a long garland. The easy braided basket adds a bright country touch to your home long after the Easter eggs are gone.

And you'll find a useful Bunny and Carrot Chatelaine that can be draped around your neck to keep sewing tools handy. There's a fat felt bunny pincushion on one end and scissors snuggled inside a carrot pocket on the other end. (A small, clean stone can be inserted inside the bunny to balance the weight of the scissors.) Use a good sturdy felt and save the scraps to make some extra bunnies just for fun!

EGG BUNNY GARLAND

Materials for one four-bunny unit
Pattern on page 43
3½" x 7" piece of medium-weight white paper
4 (1½" x 2¼") scraps of colored stationery-weight paper
Craft knife
⅛" paper punch
Black fine-point marker
Rubber cement
White glue

Instructions
1. Trace pattern pieces, transferring markings. Cut out.

2. Referring to Diagram, score white paper on all fold lines (see Figure A) and accordian-fold (see Figure B). Tape folded paper to protected work surface. Place bunny pattern on paper, aligning edges of pattern with folds. Trace pattern, remove, and cut through all layers. *Do not cut folds (see pattern markings).* Unfold, transfer features to each bunny, and draw features with marker.

3. Stack colored papers and tape to protected work surface. Trace vest pattern on top sheet and cut through all layers. (Check fit on 1 bunny and trim, if necessary.)

Apply thin layer of rubber cement to center front of each bunny and to back of each vest. Let dry. Referring to pattern, carefully join 1 vest to each bunny (dry cement will bond on contact). Rub off excess cement with fingertips.

4. Punch 3 holes for buttons from each remaining colored paper scrap. Glue buttons to each vest.

BRAIDED BASKET

Materials
⅝ yard of madras fabric
11 yards (⅜") of cotton filler cord
Thread to match
Bodkin or large safety pin
Masking tape
Rubber bands
Large sturdy needle
Note: This basket may also be made from 3 (1⅞" x 132") strips pieced from assorted scrap fabrics.

Instructions
1. From madras, cut 9 (1⅞" x 44") strips. Join 3 strips to make 1 (132"-long) pieced strip. Repeat to make 2 more pieced strips.

2. Refer to Steps 1–2 for Braided Nest, page 14, to make fabric-covered tubes.

3. Align 3 tubes at 1 end and stitch together. Roll up extra tube yardage and secure each bundle with a rubber band. Tape or pin unit to work surface and make a flat braid, unrolling bundles as needed. Secure ends with a rubber band. Cut 14"-long piece of braid for handle, fastening each cut end with rubber band. Set aside.

4. To make basket base, lay stitched end of braid flat on work surface. Keeping 6½" of braid flat, begin to coil braid to make a flat oval. Slipstitch edges of braid together as you work. After flat oval has been formed, build basket sides by stacking remaining braid on edge as you coil. (To check shape, pin or tape stacked braids together before you stitch.) At end of braid, remove rubber bands, tuck raw ends inside fabric tubes, and slipstitch to inside of basket.

5. For handle, remove rubber bands from reserved braid. Trim cord at each end ½" shorter than tube; tack cord ends to tube. Pull fabric back down over cord. Referring to photo, pin handle in place. Tuck each cut end under coils inside basket and slipstitch securely.

Diagram: Folding White Paper

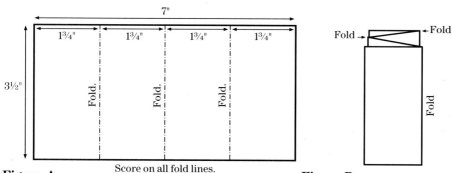

Figure A — Score on all fold lines.   **Figure B**

BUNNY AND CARROT CHATELAINE

Materials

Pattern on pages 43–44
5" x 8" piece of white felt for bunny, ears, and base
1½" x 5" piece of pink felt for inner bunny ears
8" x 10" piece of light orange felt for carrot
1¾ yards (⅜"-wide) of green picot-edged ribbon
Thread to match
Embroidery floss: white, pink, orange
1 (¾") white pom-pom
5" scissors with orange handles
Straight pins with colored heads
Vanishing fabric marker

Instructions for bunny

1. Trace pattern pieces, transferring markings. Cut out.

2. On white felt, trace 1 ear piece, 1 base, and 2 body pieces, transferring markings, including stitching line on body pieces. Cut out base and body pieces. *Do not cut out ears yet.*

Pin uncut ear piece to pink felt and baste layers together within shape. Cutting through both layers, cut out ear piece.

3. Across bottom of each body piece, machine-staystitch along seam line. (This is essential.) With raw edges aligned, pin body pieces together and machine-stitch, leaving bottom open. Trim seam allowance, except along opening, and clip curves. Turn right side out and stuff firmly.

4. Matching dots, pin and baste to bottom of bunny body. Using 3 strands of white floss, attach base to body with small blanket stitches.

5. Using 3 strands of white floss, make small blanket stitches around ear piece. Fold ears in half lengthwise and stitch folded layers together at center, as indicated on pattern. Tack ears to head at dots.

Curl ears forward or backward and tack upright or down, as desired.

6. Tack pom-pom to center back, as indicated on pattern. To shape head, stitch back and forth in eye area through sides of head; pull thread tightly and tie off. For eyes, use 3 strands of pink floss to make French knots.

Instructions for carrot

1. Trace pattern pieces, transferring markings. Cut out.

2. From orange felt, cut 1 carrot piece and 1 lining piece, transferring markings.

3. Pin long straight edges of carrot piece together and machine-stitch. Referring to Diagram 1, rotate seam to center back and flatten. At bottom edge, machine-stitch straight across. Trim bottom seam allowance only to ⅟₁₆". Without allowing stitches to go through to front, slipstitch center seam allowances to carrot. Carefully turn right side out. Do not stretch.

4. For lining, repeat Step 3, except turn long seam to *front* as shown in Diagram 2. Do not turn lining right side out. Insert lining into carrot, gently pushing it down with eraser

Diagram 1: Making Carrot

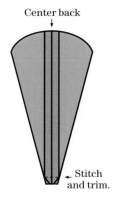

Center back

Stitch and trim.

Diagram 2: Making Lining

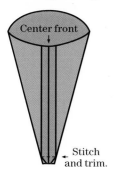

Center front

Stitch and trim.

end of pencil. Align raw edges, matching dots with seams.

5. Cut 45" of ribbon. Tack 1 end to carrot seam allowance between layers at center back. On other end of ribbon, slipstitch a narrow hem and tack to bunny at mouth area.

6. For carrot greens, cut 3 (6") lengths from remaining ribbon. Fold 1 length in half and baste cut edges

together. Repeat to make 3 loops. Tack basted ends to carrot seam allowance between layers at center back. Baste cut edges of carrot and lining together. Using 3 strands of orange floss, blanket-stitch around basted edges, catching ends of ribbon loops in stitches.

Place pins in bunny pincushion and insert scissors into carrot.

COUNTRY ACCENT

Use a bit of old-fashioned country ingenuity to turn pressed-paper egg cartons into decorative Easter baskets. And, of course, you'll want to save the contents of the eggs for baking. (To prevent contamination, remember to keep all unwrapped food away from the egg carton, the eggshells, and any straw that is used in the basket.)

With a very sharp craft knife, cut the lid from the carton and set it aside. If the carton bottom has an extension along the front edge, trim and discard it. From one end of the carton bottom, cut a cross section that holds four eggs. From the other end, cut a section that holds two eggs. Glue the cut ends together to form a basket. Discard the center section.

For a handle, cut a straight 10"-long strip from the carton lid and glue each end on the inside of opposite sides of the basket. Line the basket with a thin layer of straw.

To empty the eggshells, use a large needle to make a hole in one end; enlarge the hole to about ½". Break the yolk with the needle and shake the liquid contents into a bowl. Rinse out the eggshells and let them dry.

Decorate the eggshells with a sponge dipped in undiluted food coloring. Or fill the shells with potting soil and plant tiny seedlings.

MOTHER'S DAY KEEPSAKES

◆

These sentimental creations in soft spring colors make gifts that will be treasured. Fill the Sunbonnet Baby Sachet with delicious fragrance or use your smallest scraps and tiniest stitches to fashion the Sunbonnet Baby Pin.

The patchwork fan keeps notepaper and stamps tucked inside. Sewing necessities are hidden within the soft fabric heart that unfolds when the ribbons are untied. And with country-style ticking peeking through eyelet pillowcases, a pair of tiny scented pillows makes a heart-warming gift.

SUNBONNET BABY SACHET

Materials for one sachet
Pattern on page 45
5¼" x 7½" piece of print fabric for arms/dress
1" x 7½" piece of fabric for hands
4½" square of fabric for feet
7" (⅝"-wide) of ruffled eyelet lace
7" (3½"-wide) of flat eyelet edging with 1"-wide scallops for bonnet
12" (⅛"-wide) of satin ribbon
Thread to match
Polyester stuffing
Extra-fine unwaxed dental floss
Dried lavender flowers or potpourri
Note: See Resources, page 159.

Instructions
1. Trace pattern pieces, transferring markings. Cut out.
2. From print, cut a 2" x 7½" strip for arms. With right sides facing and raw edges aligned, stitch print strip to 1" x 7½" strip of hand fabric along 1 long edge. Press seam toward darker fabric.

Cut arm/hand unit in half widthwise to make 2 (2½" x 3¾") units. With right sides facing, fold 1 unit in half widthwise to measure 2½" x 1⅞". Place sachet arm/hand pattern on fold and align dotted line with seam, as indicated on pattern. Trace pattern. Repeat with remaining arm/hand unit. *Do not cut out yet.*

3. Machine-stitch along traced line on 1 unit, leaving open where indicated on pattern. Cut out, adding ¼" seam allowance. Trim stitched seam allowance to ⅛". Clip curve and turn. Stuff lightly. Flatten arm/hand with seam aligned along 1 side. Baste opening closed. Repeat for other arm/hand. Set aside.

4. Place sachet dress pattern on wrong side of remaining dress fabric and trace 2 dress pieces, ½" apart, transferring markings. Cut out, adding ¼" seam allowances.

On right side of 1 dress piece, aligning all raw edges, baste each arm/hand unit in place between marked dots. With right sides facing and raw edges aligned, machine-stitch dress pieces together along side seams, catching basted edges of arm/hand units in seams. Turn dress right side out.

With right sides facing and aligning bound edge of ruffled lace with bottom raw edge of dress, handstitch lace to dress. Set aside.

5. For feet, fold fabric square in half with right sides facing. Place pattern on fold and trace 2 foot pieces. *Do not cut out yet.* Follow Step 3 to complete 2 feet, omitting basting open edges. With open edges aligned, stack feet pointing in same direction. Baste feet together along open edges.

6. On dress/arm unit, rotate side seams to center as shown in Diagram. Place feet on seam as shown and baste to 1 layer of dress/lace at bottom. Tucking feet inside, turn entire unit wrong side out. Center seams again, pin open bottom edges together, and machine-stitch, catching tops of feet in seam. Turn unit right side out.

Fold under ¼" along neck edge. Thread needle with dental floss and, starting at X (see Diagram), run gathering stitches around neckline 1/16" from folded neck edge. *Do not gather yet.* Leaving 3" tails of floss, remove needle. Loosely fill dress with lavender or potpourri. Set aside.

7. For bonnet, fold eyelet edging in half widthwise, with right sides facing and scallops aligned along front edge (see pattern). Place pattern on fold and trace. Cut out, adding ¼" seam allowance. Stitch center back seam, leaving neck edge open. Trim and clip seam; turn. Topstitch bonnet where indicated on pattern. Lightly stuff bonnet with polyester stuffing and flatten with center back seam aligned along 1 side. Stitch bottom edges together.

Aligning folds at back of bonnet and back of dress, tuck bottom seam allowance of bonnet inside neckline of dress and pin together. Whipstitch units together around neckline, avoiding catching dental floss in stitching. Pull tails of floss to gather neckline to 1⅛" and tie off.

Stitching through both layers of bonnet, run gathering stitches along topstitching line from top of head to neckline. Pull thread to gather to 1½". Tie off. Tie ribbon in a bow around neck.

Diagram: Rotating Seams and Adding Feet

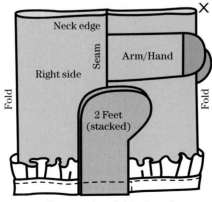

Bottom edge of skirt (open)

SUNBONNET BABY PIN OR MAGNET

Materials for one baby
Pattern on page 45
3½" x 4½" scrap of fabric for
   arms/dress
1" x 4½" scrap of fabric for hands
3¼" square of fabric for feet
4" (½"-wide) of ruffled lace
3½" (2"-wide) of flat eyelet edging
   with ½"-wide scallops for bonnet
9" (1/16"-wide) of satin ribbon
Thread to match
Polyester stuffing
Extra-fine unwaxed dental floss
Safety pin (for pin) *or* magnetic tape
   (for magnet)

Instructions
1. From dress fabric, cut a 1⅜" x
4½" strip for arms. Referring to
Steps 1–3 of Sunbonnet Baby Sachet,
page 30, assemble arm/hand units,
using tiny handstitches instead of
machine-stitching and trimming
seams to 1/16".
2. Referring to Steps 4–7, complete
Sunbonnet Baby, using polyester
stuffing in skirt instead of potpourri.
Gather neckline to ¾" and bonnet
to ⅞".
3. Sew safety pin to center back or
add narrow strip of magnetic tape.

*Once opened,
the Fan Note Holder
provides roomy pock-
ets. A small Velcro dot
helps keep stationery
and stamps secure.*

FAN NOTE HOLDER

Materials
Pattern on page 46
9" x 13½" piece of green print fabric
9" x 23" piece of floral print fabric
9" x 17½" piece of orchid pindot
   fabric for lining
4" square of beige pindot fabric
34" (½"-wide) of scalloped lace
Thread to match
9" x 17½" piece of thin quilt batting
Vanishing fabric marker
1 (½"-diameter) white Velcro dot

Instructions
1. Trace pattern pieces, transferring markings. Cut out.
2. Trace and cut pieces as indicated on pattern, adding ¼" seam allowances. On right side of each floral
print A (pocket pieces), lightly
transfer topstitching line and fold

line for hem.
3. To make fan patchwork, with right
sides facing and raw edges aligned,
join 1 green print B and 1 floral print
B together along 1 straight edge.
Press seam open. Alternating prints,
join remaining Bs together along
straight edge, forming fan shape. On
right side of patchwork, along
curved base of fan, lightly draw a
line ¼" from raw edge.
   Cut 6½" of lace and align bound
edge of lace along marked line on
fan, with scallops pointing away
from base. Baste. Clip seam allowance almost to marked line. With
right sides facing and raw edges
aligned, pin beige pindot C to patchwork fan along clipped curve, easing
fabric to fit. Machine-stitch, catching
basted edge of lace in stitching. Clip
curve and press seam allowance toward C.

4. With right sides facing and raw edges aligned, machine-stitch green print A to patchwork fan along left straight edge. Press seam open. On right side of front/back unit, with fan on right side, back on left side, and straight edge at bottom, lightly draw a line ¼" away from curved edge. Align bound edge of remaining lace along marked line, with scallops pointing toward lower part of fan. Baste and set aside.

5. For pocket, on 1 floral print A, turn raw edge under ¼" on side marked with stars; then turn under on marked fold line. Press. Trim excess fabric at top to match curved top edge. Machine-stitch pressed hem. Repeat with remaining floral print A.

Stack batting and lining (right side up). Align 1 pocket (right side up) on each side. Pin and baste through all layers. Topstitch each pocket through all layers along marked line, backstitching at hemmed edge.

6. With right sides facing and raw edges, center seam, and center fold aligned, pin pocket/lining/batting unit and patchwork front/back unit together. Baste.

Beginning on straight bottom edge, machine-stitch around shape, leaving 4" opening along straight edge for turning. Trim excess batting ⅛" from raw edges, except for ¼" along opening. Clip curves, trim corners, and turn right side out. Slipstitch opening closed.

7. Press lightly. Using thread in bobbin to match lining, topstitch in-the-ditch along center seam of patchwork front/back. Referring to pattern for placement, slipstitch Velcro dot halves to inside of folder, through 1 layer only.

HEART MENDER SEWING KIT

Materials
Pattern on page 47
9 (5¾") squares of stripe fabric
Note: Cut each square with a stripe running down center.
3" x 5" piece of linen or flannel for needle keeper
60" (¼"-wide) of coordinating satin ribbon
Thread: to match stripe fabric and ribbon, 8 assorted colors for posterboard bobbin
Embroidery floss to match stripe fabric
Vanishing fabric marker
3 (6" x 10") pieces of posterboard
Rubber cement
Craft knife
⅛" paper punch
Small safety pins, glass-headed straight pins, and needles

Instructions
1. On folded paper, trace patterns A, B, and C, transferring markings. Cut out. On flat paper, trace patterns D, E, and F, transferring markings. Cut out.

2. On wrong side of 4 fabric squares, trace 1 A, aligning a stripe down center of each heart and transferring markings. Cut out.

3. For pocket, on wrong side of 1 fabric square, with stripes running horizontally, trace 1 B. Transfer markings and cut out. Fold along hemline, baste, and machine-stitch. With wrong side of pocket facing right side of 1 A and raw edges aligned, baste together.

4. With right sides facing and center stripes aligned, pin 1 A to 1 fabric square. Stitch around top of heart from dot to dot, leaving open below. Trim fabric square to match heart shape; then trim seam allowance in stitched area to ⅛". Clip curves and crevice at top of heart. Repeat with remaining hearts and fabric squares.

5. Turn all heart units right side out. Below stitched seams on each heart unit, fold under seam allowances and baste, leaving bottom of each heart unit open. Set aside.

Continued on page 34

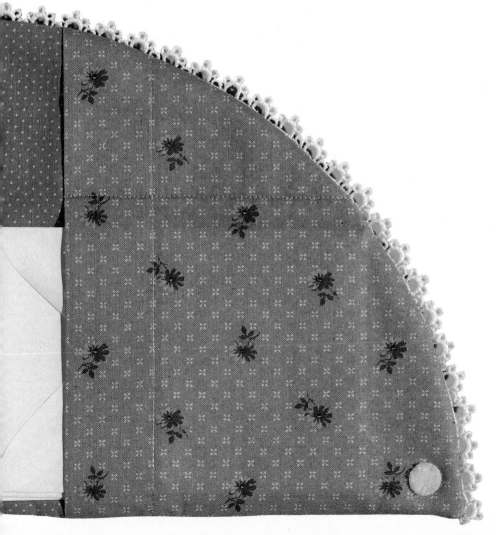

Continued from page 33

6. Spread thin layer of rubber cement on 2 pieces of posterboard. When dry, align edges and press together. Trace 2 Cs on doubled posterboard and cut out.

On remaining piece of posterboard, trace 4 Ds and cut out. Reserve scraps.

7. Insert 1 posterboard C inside heart/pocket unit and 1 additional heart unit. Set aside.

To make folding hearts, align basted open edges of 1 heart unit and pin together. At tip, securely tack layers together, as invisibly as possible. With marker, draw center line from crevice to tip of heart. Beside this line, baste layers together. Beginning and ending with backstitches, machine-stitch along marked line. Insert 1 posterboard D into each half of heart, trimming D along center, if necessary. Repeat with remaining folding heart unit.

Slipstitch open edges of all heart units closed.

8. To add accessories, cut 2 (5½") lengths of ribbon and, referring to photo, cross ribbons on 1 folding heart; pin in place. Tuck cut ends of each ribbon under and slipstitch to heart along edge. Repeat with remaining folding heart.

Referring to photo, place all hearts on flat work surface, alternating solid hearts and folding hearts. (Pocket side on 1 solid heart should be face down and ribbon side of folding hearts should be face up.) Stack 2 adjacent hearts with right sides facing. Starting at tip, make tiny whipstitches along 2" of 1 straight edge. Tie off securely.

Repeat to join 2 remaining single hearts; then repeat to join all hearts together.

9. For bobbin, trace 1 E on posterboard scrap, transferring markings. Cut out. Cut slits and punch hole where indicated. Score fold lines and fold.

Anchoring ends of threads in slits, wrap 4 colors of thread around each side of bobbin. For hanger, cut 3 (9")

lengths of floss; align and tie lengths together at 1 end. Braid floss and thread through hole in bobbin. With single strand of thread, tie ends of thread together. Extending ends of braid slightly over top of 1 solid heart, slipstitch braid securely to heart.

10. For needle keeper, trace 1 F on linen or flannel and cut out. Using 3 strands of floss, make blanket stitches around edge. Center on heart opposite bobbin and tack in place along top edge.

11. Cut remaining length of ribbon in half. Turn 1 cut end of 1 length under ½" and slipstitch to top of heart with bobbin, covering ends of floss braid. Repeat with remaining length of ribbon at top of opposite heart.

Insert pins and needles as shown in photo. To fold kit, bring folding hearts to center, pulling solid hearts toward each other. Tie ribbons together at top.

U*ntie the satin ribbons and find thread, pins, and needles tucked into the Heart Mender Sewing Kit.*

li]

HERBAL PILLOWS

Materials for two pillows
2 (4½" x 10¼") pieces of pillow
  ticking, cut with stripes
  parallel to 4½" edge
2 (5¾" x 9") pieces of eyelet edging,
  cut with scallops on 9" edge
44" (¼"-wide) of lavender satin
  ribbon
Thread to match
Dried lavender flowers or
  potpourri*

Cream satin ribbon rose with leaves
  (optional)
Dried flowers (optional)
*Note: See Resources, page 159.

Instructions
  1. With right sides facing and raw
edges aligned, fold 1 piece of pillow
ticking in half widthwise to measure
4½" x 5⅛".
  Machine-stitch around raw edges,
leaving 2" opening. Turn pillow right
side out. Fill with lavender flowers
or potpourri. Slipstitch opening

closed. Repeat for remaining pillow.
  2. For pillowcases, with right sides
facing and raw edges aligned, fold 1
piece of edging in half widthwise to
measure 5¾" x 4½".
  Machine-stitch along raw edges,
leaving scalloped edge open. Turn
right side out and finger-press.
Repeat for other pillowcase.
  3. Insert pillows in cases. Stack
pillows and tie together with ribbon.
Tack satin rose to bow and add dried
flowers, if desired.

LAZY DAYS

School's out! Summer's in! The screen door slams as we go out on the porch to savor the long Lazy Days. Hang the flag, pack a picnic, work in the garden, play ball, rest in a hammock, and count the clouds. Summertime symbols of pinwheels, flags, and stars decorate this chapter's projects for special events or just for fun.

MEMOO

Milk
Butter

HAPPY DAYS!

◆

Celebrate the end of another school year by recycling the cover of a well-used composition notebook to make a cheerful Memoo Board. And carry on the black-and-white color scheme with crisp fabric pinwheels, easy magnets made from dominoes and dice, a pinwheel pot holder, and a gathered apron swirling with big polka dots.

MEMOO BOARD

Materials
Pattern on page 72
2 (4½" x 6½") pieces of black-and-white notebook cover cardboard
1½" x 4" scrap of black-and-white paper peeled from notebook cardboard
Craft knife
4½"-long pencil
32" (⅛"-wide) of black grosgrain ribbon
9½" (⅛"-wide) of black-with-white dot grosgrain ribbon
White glue
1½" x 2" white self-sticking notepad
Black fine-point marker
4 (¾") black buttons

Instructions
1. Trace pattern and cut out. On 1 scrap of cardboard, trace 1 cow and cut out. Reverse pattern and trace 1 on remaining scrap; cut out. Glue wrong sides of cows together and press under books until dry.

To cover pencil, glue peeled paper around pencil, trimming excess if necessary.

2. Starting and ending at back of cow, glue black ribbon completely around edge of cow, leaving 11" unattached for tail. Glue end of ribbon around unsharpened end of pencil.

If desired, trace "MEMOO" letters and transfer to top page of pad with black marker. Glue pad to cow. Glue 1 button to base of each leg on each side of cow. Tie dotted ribbon in bow around cow's neck.

DOMINO AND DICE MAGNETS

Materials for two magnets
2 dominoes or dice
2 small magnets
Craft glue

Instructions
Glue 1 magnet to back of each domino or dice.

FABRIC PINWHEEL

Materials for one large pinwheel
Pattern on page 72
2 (5½") squares of different
    black-and-white print fabrics
2 (5½") squares of paperbacked
    fusible web
Black thread
5½" square of paper
Liquid ravel preventer
Darning needle
1 (½") white button
12" (¼"-diameter) dowel
Craft glue
Note: This decorative pinwheel does
    not rotate.

Instructions
1. Trace pattern, transferring markings. Cut out.

2. Following manufacturer's instructions, fuse 1 fabric square to paper square. Fuse remaining fabric square to other side of paper and apply liquid ravel preventer to all edges. Let dry. Transfer pattern markings to 1 side, using darning needle to pierce dots. Cut blades of pinwheel.

3. Place a pin through hole on 1 blade; then, in sequence, add remaining blades on pin, folding corners with holes to center. Push pin through center of square and stitch all layers together at center. Remove pin. Stitch or glue button in center. Using black thread, stitch through holes of button. Glue center of pinwheel to top of dowel.

MINI-PINWHEEL PIN OR MAGNET

Materials for one mini-pinwheel
Pattern on page 72
2 (1¾") squares of different
    black-and-white print fabrics
1¾" square of paperbacked
    fusible web
Black thread
Darning needle
1 (¼") black button
Liquid ravel preventer
Craft glue
Round toothpick
1" pin fastener *or* small magnet

Instructions
1. Trace pattern, transferring
markings. Cut out.
2. Refer to Steps 2–3 of Fabric
Pinwheel at left, omitting paper and
using toothpick instead of dowel.
3. Glue magnet or pin fastener to
center back of pinwheel.

PINWHEEL POT HOLDER

Materials
Pattern on page 73
10" square of black-and-white stripe
    fabric
5" x 7" piece of black-with-white dot
    fabric
4" x 10" piece of black-and-white
    check fabric
5" x 7" piece of white fabric
8" square of black fabric for backing
5" (¼"-wide) of black double-fold bias
    tape
Thread to match
8" square of thick quilt batting
1 (¾") black button (optional)
White embroidery floss (optional)

Instructions
1. Trace pattern pieces, transferring markings. Cut out.
2. Cut out fabrics as indicated on
patterns.
3. Referring to Diagram, assemble
patchwork. Press seams open.
4. Stack batting; backing (right
side up); and patchwork square
(right side down). Pin layers together. Machine-stitch around edges,
leaving 3" opening for turning. Trim
excess batting. Clip corners and
turn. Press edges gently and pin
layers together. Stitch in-the-ditch
along seam line of the borders
around pinwheel.
5. For hanger loop, slipstitch bias
tape together along folded edge. Fold
tape in half to form loop and tack
ends to back of pot holder at 1 corner. If desired, use embroidery floss
to tack button at center of pinwheel.

Diagram: Assembling Patchwork

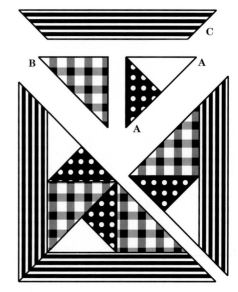

POLKA-DOT APRON

Materials
1 yard of white-with-black-dot fabric
4⅞ yards (½"-wide) of black
    double-fold bias tape
Thread to match
Vanishing fabric marker
White dressmaker's pencil
Large safety pin or bodkin

Instructions
  1. Referring to Diagram 1, use fabric marker to trace measurements and markings on wrong side of fabric. Cut out apron square and casing, reserving large scrap for another use.
  2. On 2 opposite side edges of apron square, turn raw edges under ¼" twice to back; press and then machine-stitch each side. Cut 37" of bias tape and turn each cut edge under ½"; then bind bottom raw edge of apron square.
  To make casing, turn each short end of casing strip under ½"; press and stitch. Press each long raw edge under ¼", but do not stitch. On wrong side of apron, aligning short ends of casing with sides of apron, pin casing along placement line. Machine-stitch casing to apron along each long edge.
  3. For drawstring, cut 72" of bias tape and turn each end under ½". Machine-stitch along all edges. Pull drawstring through casing with safety pin or bodkin, but do not gather yet.
  4. Along top edge of apron, run 2 rows of gathering stitches, ¼" and ⅜" from top. Pull thread to gather top to 12". Cut 66" of bias tape, fold in half widthwise, and use white pencil to mark center. On each side of center point, measure 6" and mark. Insert gathered edges of apron top within this 12" area and pin. Referring to Diagram 2, make mitered corners on *front* of apron at each end; baste folds. Turn bias tape under ½" at each cut end. Machine-stitch along open edge of tape, catching gathered apron top in stitching. Then machine-stitch along folded edges and each mitered corner. Pull drawstring to gather waistline.

Diagram 1: Cutting Apron and Casing

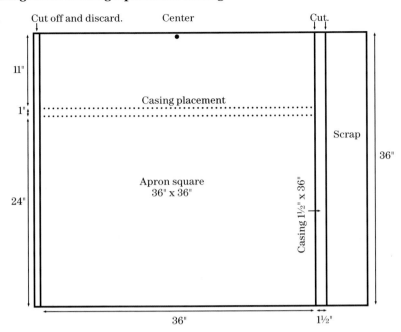

Cut off and discard.   Center   Cut.

11"

Casing placement

1"

Scrap

36"

24"

Apron square
36" x 36"

Casing 1½" x 36"

36"   1½"

**Diagram 2:
Making Mitered Corners**

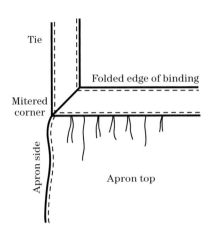

Tie

Folded edge of binding

Mitered
corner

Apron side

Apron top

COUNTRY ACCENT

Summertime brings simple pleasures, like a weekend breakfast on the patio. Dress up your table easily with bandanna napkins and napkin rings made quickly from big buttons and thin cable cord.

For each napkin ring, cut 16" of cord. Working from the back to the front, thread each end of the cord through adjacent holes in a large button. Crisscross the cord on the front of the button and thread each end through the remaining holes to the back. Tie a knot 1" from each end and fringe the ends. Insert a bandanna napkin and slide the button on the cord to adjust the fit.

HAVE A BALL

◆

A big beach ball is just right for rolling along the porch floor for a toddler to chase. Use scraps of a strong, tightly woven fabric and *lots* of stuffing to make it really roly-poly!

The fabric softball has two interlocking pieces that may be cut from scraps of the same fabric or from two different prints. You can even simulate the softball stitching with hand embroidery, if you like.

BEACH BALL

Materials
Pattern on page 73
6 (4½" x 11") pieces of fabric for
    segments
2 (2½") squares of fabric for ends
Thread to match
Polyester stuffing

Instructions
1. Trace pattern pieces, transferring markings. Cut out.

2. On wrong side of each 4½" x 11" piece of fabric, trace segment pattern. Transfer dots to 1 segment. On wrong side of each 2½" square, trace end circle pattern. Adding ¼" seam allowance, cut out all pieces.

On each segment, machine-staystitch short curved ends along seam line. With right sides facing and raw edges aligned, pin pairs of segments together. Backstitching at beginning and end, machine-stitch pairs together, leaving open between large dots on 1 pair. Join all pairs together to form ball.

3. Trim seam allowances to ⅛" along all stitched seams; leave ¼" along open edges. Clip curves and turn.

4. Stuff very firmly through opening. Slipstitch opening closed.

5. On each end circle, clip seam allowance, turn under, and baste. Pin circles to ball at ends and slipstitch securely.

FABRIC SOFTBALL

Materials for one ball
Pattern on page 74
2 (3¾" x 11") pieces of fabric
Polyester stuffing
Thread to match
Embroidery floss (optional)

Instructions

1. Trace pattern, transferring markings, and cut out.

2. On wrong side of each fabric piece, trace pattern, transferring markings. Adding ¼" seam allowance, cut out. Clip seam allowance almost to seam line at ¼" intervals.

3. With right sides facing and all dots matching, pin pieces together. Baste carefully, close to seam line. Machine-stitch seam, leaving 2" opening between small dots along 1 edge. Clip seam allowance again. If desired, push seam allowance toward darker fabric and baste to secure until ball is stuffed.

4. Turn right side out. Turn each seam allowance under at opening and baste to inside. Stuff ball firmly, molding it into a sphere. Slipstitch opening closed. (To smooth seam, test fabric for color-fastness and then dampen seam with wet washcloth and let dry.)

5. If desired, after seam is dry, use 6 strands of floss to embroider angled straight stitches along seam.

FATHER'S DAY SURPRISES

◆

Instead of buying your dad another new tie, turn some of his well-worn old clothes into Bow Tie Mini-Pillows. Filled with fragrant balsam fir tips or cedar chips, the aroma will remind him of an early-morning walk in the woods.

And make a unique set of bookends from an ordinary pair of work gloves. On one glove, tack the thumb to one finger and tuck in an extra surprise, like a seed packet or two, a paintbrush, or a carpenter's pencil. You'll know just the right touch to let Dad know that you made this gift especially for him.

BOW TIE MINI-PILLOW

Materials for one pillow
Pattern on page 74
3" x 5" piece of shirt fabric
5" square of necktie silk
4" square of muslin or batiste
7" x 14" piece of dark menswear
   fabric
Neutral thread
4 (³⁄₈") shirt collar buttons
Balsam fir tips or cedar chips
Note: See Resources, page 159.

Instructions
1. Trace pattern pieces, transferring markings. Cut out.

2. Trace and cut pieces as indicated on pattern. On right side of 2 shirt fabric Bs, transfer dots for button placement. From menswear fabric, cut a 5½" square for pillow back.

3. Referring to photo and Diagram, Figure A, and stitching only from corner dot to corner dot, join 2 necktie silk Bs to opposite sides of A. Repeat to join 2 shirt fabric Bs to A. Stitch adjacent edges of Bs together from dot to outside edges. Press block. On wrong side of block, baste C. Referring to dots for placement, sew 2 buttons on each shirt fabric B.

4. Referring to Figure B and ending stitching at corner dot of B, add 1 D. Press seam toward border. Referring to Figure C, add remaining Ds, finishing by stitching short end of last strip joined to edge of first strip from corner dot to outside edge.

5. With right sides facing and raw edges aligned, pin patchwork block to pillow back. Machine-stitch around edges, leaving 1½" opening for turning. Clip corners and turn right side out. Fill with balsam or cedar. Slipstitch opening closed.

WORK GLOVE BOOKENDS

Materials
Pattern on page 75
1 pair of men's heavyweight cotton
   work gloves
4³⁄₈" x 6" pair of heavy-gauge steel
   bookends (available at stationery
   stores)
2 (5½" x 10") pieces of lightweight
   cardboard
Craft knife

Instructions
1. Trace pattern and compare to glove. Adjust length or width to fit, if necessary.

2. On cardboard, trace insert pattern, transferring markings. Cut out. Score center line. Fold and insert cardboard into glove. Unfold cardboard and fit into fingers of glove. Slip glove over bookend. Repeat with remaining glove. Add accessories, if desired.

*W*ork Glove Bookends (left) are easily made from a new pair of cotton gloves, while the Bow Tie Mini-Pillows (center) are stitched from Dad's old ties and shirts.

**Diagram:
Assembling Bow Tie Mini-Pillow Top**

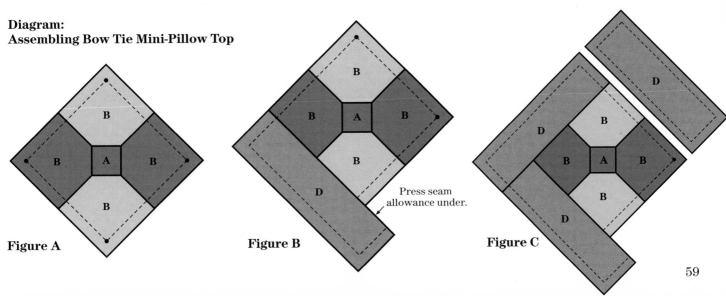

Figure A

Figure B

Press seam allowance under.

Figure C

59

SALUTE THE RED, WHITE, AND BLUE!

◆

Host a flag-waving picnic on the Fourth of July and sport stars and stripes all summer long. The rickrack flag waves on sweatshirts and the easy apron. Make star-shaped pillows that shine in bright bandanna prints or sparkle with silvery trim. Fashion a folksy flag from red, white, and blue bandannas or make a patriotic patchwork pillow.

RICKRACK FLAG OR APPLIQUÉ

Materials
Pattern on pages 76–77
6¼" x 9¾" piece of red fabric
6¼" x 9¾" piece for backing (for flag)
6" square of navy fabric
48" of white jumbo rickrack
Thread to match
White dressmaker's pencil
Transparent tape
White round or star-shaped buttons:
  8 (⁹⁄₁₆") for Field A
  12 (⁹⁄₁₆") for Field B
  15 (⁵⁄₁₆") for Field C
15" (¼"-diameter) dowel (for flag)

Instructions
   1. Trace field A, B, or C pattern and flag background pattern, transferring markings. Cut out.
   2. On right side of red fabric, use white pencil to draw flag and lightly transfer placement markings for field and stripes.
   From rickrack, cut 3 (6¼"-long) strips and 3 (9¾"-long) strips. Place 1 long strip across red fabric at base of field area, aligning rickrack peaks with marked line and 1 valley with dot at corner of field (see pattern). Tape rickrack in place. Position remaining strips, aligning peaks of rickrack with marked lines and creating a consistent "wave" pattern (see photo). Machine-stitch along center of each strip, removing tape as you sew. Trim excess rickrack.
   3. To make field, on right side of navy fabric, center selected field pattern. Use white pencil to transfer button placement dots and seam line. Stitch buttons in place.
   Cut out field. Press seam allowance under ¼" along right and lower edges. Pin field in place on flag and slipstitch folded edges to flag. Baste cut edges together.
   4. Cut out flag. With right sides facing, pin top to backing and machine-stitch around edges, leaving 2" opening for turning. Trim backing to match flag. Clip corners, turn right side out, and press. Glue left side of flag to top of dowel.
   5. For appliqué, omit backing and press ¼" seam allowances under on all sides of flag.

RICKRACK FLAG SWEATSHIRT

Materials
Rickrack flag appliqué
Adult sweatshirt
Thread to match

Instructions
   Following label directions, wash and dry sweatshirt. Position appliqué and pin to shirt. Slipstitch in place.

Y̲ou'll want to
use these easy-to-stitch all-
American accessories for
all the summer patriotic
holidays: Memorial Day,
Flag Day, and the Fourth of
July. From back left:
Rickrack Flag Sweatshirt
and Adjustable Apron; cen-
ter: Bandanna Star Pillow,
Trimmed Star Pillow, and
Rickrack Flag.

ADJUSTABLE APRON

Materials
Pattern on page 75
1 yard of sturdy white fabric
Thread to match
4 yards (1"-wide) of white twill tape
Rickrack flag appliqué
Vanishing fabric marker
Large safety pin

Instructions
1. On folded paper, trace apron facing pattern, transferring markings. Cut out.

2. From white fabric, cut 30" x 35½" rectangle for apron. On remaining scrap, trace facing pattern twice and cut out. Along outer curved edge of each facing, press under ¼" and stitch. Along each short end, press under ¾" and stitch. Set aside.

3. To hem sides of apron, turn each long edge of rectangle under ¼" and press; then turn under ⅜", press again, and machine-stitch.

To hem top and bottom, turn each short edge of rectangle under ¼" and press; then turn under 1½", press again, and machine-stitch. Rectangle should measure 28¾" x 32".

4. Referring to Diagram, with right sides facing, align ends of 1 facing with top and side of rectangle, 9" from corner. Pin securely and trim rectangle to match raw edge of facing. Beginning and ending with backstitches, machine-stitch ¼" from curved raw edge of facing. Clip seam allowance. Repeat with remaining facing.

Press facings to wrong side of apron and baste. To make casings for neck loop and waist ties, machine-stitch open curved edge of each facing to apron, beginning and ending with backstitches. Inside each end of each casing, slipstitch seam allowance to facing. With large safety pin, thread length of twill tape up through 1 casing and then down through casing on other side, leaving loop of twill tape at top to go around neck. Hem each cut end of twill tape. (Before washing, remove ties.)

5. Referring to photo for placement, slipstitch rickrack flag appliqué to apron, stitching through top layer only in casing area.

Diagram: Pinning Facings

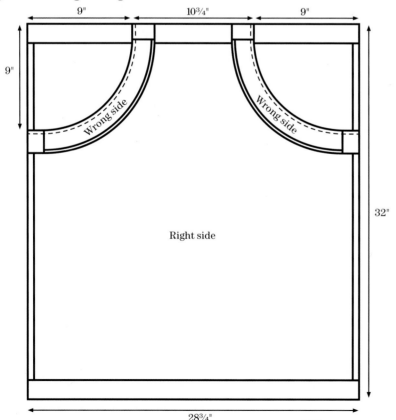

BANDANNA FLAG

Materials for one flag
Pattern on page 79
3 red bandannas, each printed with 18½"-long border
1 blue bandanna
20" x 26" piece of white opaque fabric
Neutral thread
15½" x 20" piece of thin batting (optional)
Quilting thread (optional)
2 yards of jute or twine
Twig or branch

Instructions
1. Trace field pattern on folded paper and cut out.

From white fabric, cut 15½" x 20" backing piece and set aside. From remainder, cut 3 (1⅝" x 19") strips and 3 (1⅝" x 11⅛") strips for stripes.

From red bandanna borders, cut 3 (1⅝" x 19") strips and 4 (1⅝" x 11⅛") strips for stripes.

2. Alternating color placement, join long red and white strips together along long edges. Press seams toward red strips. Set aside.

Beginning and ending with a red strip, repeat to join short red and white strips. Set aside.

3. On 1 corner of blue bandanna, trace field pattern and cut out. Repeat to cut second piece. With right sides facing and raw edges aligned, join 2 pieces together along long edge to form 8⅜" square.

4. With right sides facing and raw edges aligned, join 1 side of blue square to left edge of reserved short red/white striped unit (see photo). Press seam toward blue square.

With right sides facing, long raw edges aligned, and alternating color placement, join this unit to reserved long red/white striped unit. Press seam toward top unit.

5. Stack batting; backing (right side up); and flag (right side down). (For unquilted flag, omit batting.) Pin layers together. Machine-stitch around edges, leaving 3" opening for turning. Clip corners and turn. Press. Stitch in-the-ditch along seams.

6. From jute or twine, cut 3 (24") lengths. Securely stitch 1 each to top of flag, bottom of field, and bottom of flag. Tie flag to twig or branch.

The Bandanna Flag (right) and Variable Star Flag Pillow (left) will give patriotic flair to your front porch.

BANDANNA STAR PILLOW

Materials for one pillow
Pattern on page 79
5 (5" x 8") pieces of bandanna
Note: Each piece must have the same
symmetrical design.
Thread to match
15" square of fabric for back
Polyester stuffing

Instructions
1. Trace pattern, transferring markings. Cut out.
2. Center pattern on right side of 1 bandanna piece and trace outline of design motifs onto pattern for placement guide. On wrong side of each piece, with traced outlines on pattern aligned with design motifs on fabric, trace pattern. Add ¼" seam allowance and cut out.
3. With right sides facing and raw edges aligned, machine-stitch pieces together from side dot to center dot along straight edges. At center, trim points of seam allowance. Press each seam allowance to 1 side in same direction.
4. To complete, refer to Steps 3–4 of Trimmed Star Pillow at right.

TRIMMED STAR PILLOW

Materials for one pillow
Pattern on page 78
2 (15") squares of fabric
54" (¼"-wide) of silver braid
Thread to match
15" square of fusible, lightweight nonwoven interfacing
Polyester stuffing
Transparent tape

Instructions
1. On folded paper, trace pattern, transferring markings. Cut out.
2. Following manufacturer's instructions, fuse interfacing to wrong side of 1 fabric square. Trace pattern on interfacing and cut out, adding ¼" seam allowance.
On right side of star, transfer placement lines for braid trim. Referring to Diagram, lay trim along marked lines, holding in place with short pieces of transparent tape placed across trim. Conceal cut ends of trim under overlapping line, as shown in Diagram. Along 1 edge, machine-stitch completely around trim, removing tape as you sew. Repeat, stitching around other edge of trim.
3. For back, cut remaining fabric square in half. With right sides facing, pin halves together along 1 long edge. Leaving 3" opening in center for turning, machine-stitch along pinned edge. Press seam open.
4. With right sides facing and back seam placed vertically, center star on back. Machine-stitch around entire star. Trim backing to match star; clip curves and clip into angles. Turn star right side out through opening in back. Stuff star firmly and flatten. Slipstitch opening closed.

**Diagram:
Adding Trim**

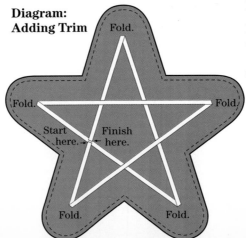

VARIABLE STAR
FLAG PILLOW

Materials for one pillow
Pattern on page 79
20" x 28½" piece of muslin
12" x 20" piece of muted red print
7" x 13" piece of muted blue print
Pieces of 3 different blue prints:
  6" x 9" piece for print #1
  4" square for print #2
  3" square for print #3
Neutral sewing thread
Polyester stuffing

Instructions
1. Trace pattern pieces, transferring markings. Cut out.
2. From muslin, cut 15½" x 20" piece for back and set aside. From remainder, cut 3 (1⅝" x 19") strips and 3 (1⅝" x 11⅛") strips for stripes; then cut 8 muslin As for patchwork.
From muted red print, cut 3 (1⅝" x 19") strips and 4 (1⅝" x 11⅛") strips for stripes.
From muted blue print, cut 2 (1⅝" x 6⅛") strips and 2 (1⅝" x 8⅜") strips for border of patchwork.
For patchwork star, cut the following: From print #1, cut 4 As and 4 Bs; from print #2, cut 4 As; from print #3, cut 1 B.
3. Referring to Diagram 1 and Fabric Key at right, assemble patchwork. Press seams toward darker fabrics. Referring to Diagram 2, add borders. Press seams toward borders. Set patchwork aside.
4. Referring to Step 2 of Bandanna Flag, page 62, assemble long and short red print/muslin striped units.
Referring to Step 4, join patchwork square and striped units.
5. With right sides facing and raw edges aligned, pin pillow front to back. Machine-stitch around edges, leaving 4" opening for turning. Clip corners and turn right side out.
Stuff pillow through opening and slipstitch opening closed.

**Diagram 1:
Assembling Star Patchwork**

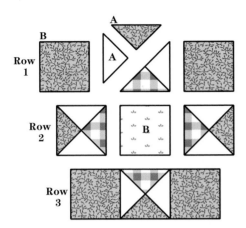

Diagram 2: Adding Borders

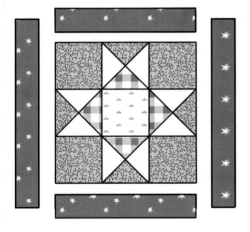

Fabric Key

 Muslin

 Blue

 Print #1

 Print #2

Print #3

COUNTRY ACCENT

Glimmering with light and shimmering with stars, an inexpensive lamp reflects the summer night sky. From a craft shop or a stationery store, purchase self-sticking stars that are about ¾" wide. Remove the shade from a small lamp. Press the stars on firmly in an even pattern around the shade or scatter randomly. (Some textured shades may require an additional dot of glue to adhere the stars.) Cover each star with a piece of clean paper and burnish well to ensure a good bond. To let the light sparkle through, pierce the center of each star with a large needle.

THE LACY DAYS OF SUMMER

◆

Long summer afternoons bring to mind lacy patterns of dappled sunlight and shadows. What a lovely time to enjoy the cool, crisp look of lace in projects that are lazy-day easy to make. You'll find cornucopias, baskets, and even vases to hold midsummer flowers.

These projects require no patterns. Sometimes, as in the Lace Curtain Shopping Bag, the design of the lace will be turned upside down, so geometric or floral patterns work best.

And if you love the look of old doilies but hate the thought of cutting them, you'll find ideas for projects made from folded doilies.

LACE CURTAIN SHOPPING BAG

Materials
1 yard of curtain or valance lace
Thread to match
40" (1"-wide) of twill tape

Instructions
1. With border design running along top edge of each piece and design motifs centered, cut 2 (17" x 18½") pieces from lace.

2. With right sides facing and all edges aligned, pin pieces together. Stitch along sides and bottom; then reinforce seams by re-stitching with zigzag stitch. Turn bag right side out.

3. For handles, cut twill tape in half. Turn under ½" on each cut end of strips and baste. Evenly space each end of 1 strip along top edge of bag, with each end extending 3" inside bag. Pin to bag; securely stitch by hand or machine. Repeat with remaining handle.

STARCHED LACE BASKET

Materials
2¾"-diameter aerosol cap or measuring cup with straight sides for basket form
10" (2"-wide) of crocheted lace
8" (½"-wide) of crocheted lace with both edges finished
2½"-diameter circle of felt to match lace for bottom
Thread to match
Spray starch

Instructions
1. With right sides facing, pin cut ends of 2"-wide lace together, forming a ring. Machine-stitch ½" from edge. Turn ring right side out. Slide on form, allowing ⅛" to overlap around bottom edge. Saturate with spray starch and let dry. Repeat several times until lace is very stiff. Leave lace ring on form.

2. For bottom of basket, slipstitch felt to overlapping bottom edge of lace. Remove basket from form.

3. For handle, place ½"-wide lace strip on protected surface and saturate with spray starch; let dry. Repeat several times. Tack each end of handle to inside of basket.

LACE VASE

Materials for one vase
5½"-high (2¾"-diameter) glass or plastic tumbler with straight sides
6" x 11" piece of lace cut with scalloped edge running along length
3" circle of washable felt (optional)
Thread to match
Note: You may use any size tumbler. Choose lace that measures ½" taller than tumbler. Trim felt circle slightly smaller than circumference of tumbler.

Instructions
1. Wrap lace around tumbler to establish length; add ½" and cut lace. With right sides facing, pin cut ends together to form a tube. Machine-stitch ¼" from edge. Turn right side out and slide on tumbler, allowing ⅛" to overlap bottom edge of tumbler if adding optional felt base. (If lace has finished bottom edge, base may be omitted.)

2. For base, slipstitch felt to overlapping bottom edge of lace.

3. To make lace fit snugly, dip lace-covered tumbler in hot water and let dry.

Display cut-tings from your summer garden in Lace Vases or add potpourri to the Starched Lace Basket (bottom left). The Lace Curtain Shopping Bag (right) is ideal for a quick trip to the market.

LACE BOW BARRETTE

Materials

6"-diameter round white crocheted doily
9" (³⁄₈"-wide) of white satin ribbon
Thread to match
3"-long (³⁄₈"-wide) metal barrette base
Craft glue
White satin ribbon rose with leaves (optional)

Instructions

1. Cut 3³⁄₄" of ribbon, reserving remainder. Center and glue ribbon to top of barrette base, folding cut ends under to back and gluing securely. Allow to dry.

2. To shape bow, pinch doily together in center; wrap thread around center to secure and tie off. Center doily on barrette base and use remaining ribbon to tie in place, knotting ribbon on back of barrette base. Trim ribbon ends. Tack rosette to ribbon at center of doily, if desired. Tack folds of doily together at center, if necessary, to maintain bow shape.

LACY BRACELET

Materials

11" (2"-wide) of white or cream bias hem facing
11" (³⁄₄"-wide) of white or cream flat crocheted lace
11" (³⁄₄"-wide) of white or cream flat crocheted lace for inside of bracelet (optional)
Thread to match
1 (³⁄₄"-wide) white or cream plastic bangle bracelet measuring 10" in circumference
Note: Adjust measurements, if necesssary, to fit your bracelet. Cut lace and bias hem facing 1" longer than circumference of bracelet.

Instructions

1. Wrap facing around bracelet and whipstitch edges together along top edge. (You can refold hem facing to adjust width, if necessary.) Turn cut ends under and slipstitch together.

2. Dip bracelet in hot water. Push seam ¹⁄₈" over top edge to outside of bracelet. Let dry.

3. Wrap lace around bracelet and whipstitch 1 long edge of lace to facing. Trim excess lace and whipstitch ends together neatly. Whipstitch remaining edge of lace to facing.

If desired, whipstitch strip of lace to facing inside bracelet along edges.

*S*mall doilies and scraps of lace become heirloom treasures with just a few stitches. Clockwise from left: Doily Sachet Pouch, Doily Basket, Eyelet Cornucopia, Mini-Cornucopia Pin or Magnet, Lacy Bracelets, Rolled Mini-Cornucopia Pin or Magnet, and Lace Bow Barrette.

EYELET CORNUCOPIA

Materials

9" (6½"-wide) of cream eyelet edging
9" (¾"-wide) of cream eyelet beading
    for handle
9" (⅜"-wide) of cream ribbon (or
    width to fit openings in beading)
Thread to match
Cream satin ribbon rose with leaves
    (optional)
Vanishing fabric marker

Instructions

1. With right sides facing, fold edging in half to measure 6½" x 4½". Mark measurements indicated in Diagram, Figure A. Draw center back seam line.

2. Stitch along line and trim seam allowance to ¼" (see Figure B). Turn right side out and rotate seam to center back, as shown in Figure C. Press.

3. For handle, weave ribbon through openings in beading. Turn cut ends under and slipstitch. Pin ends inside cornucopia at center front and 2" inside center back, covering seam; slipstitch in place. If desired, tack ribbon rose to center front.

Diagram: Making Cornucopia

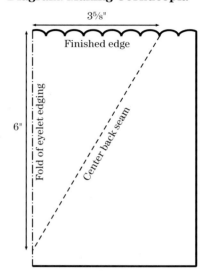

Figure A

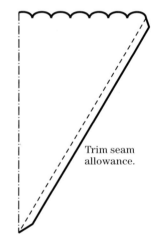

Trim seam
allowance.

Figure B

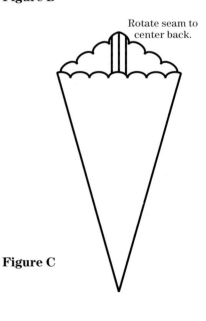

Rotate seam to
center back.

Figure C

DOILY SACHET POUCH

Materials
6"- to 8"-diameter round lace doily
  with open circular pattern
  suitable for threading ribbon
Circle of matching tulle ½" larger in
  diameter than open pattern in
  doily for threading
16" of matching ribbon to fit width of
  open pattern in doily for threading
Thread to match
Dried lavender flowers or potpourri
Note: See Resources, page 159.

Instructions
1. Run gathering stitches around
edge of tulle. Place moderate amount
of lavender or potpourri in center
and pull thread tightly to gather. Tie
off and set aside.
2. Thread ribbon around doily
through openings in lace. Place potpourri pouch in center of doily. Pull
ribbon to gather tightly; tie in bow.

DOILY CORNUCOPIA

Materials
5"- to 6"-diameter doily
6" (¼"-wide) of matching ribbon for
  handle
Thread to match
Dried flowers

Instructions
Note: Refer to photo on page 6.
1. Roll doily into cone shape and
tack along overlapped edges.
2. For handle, tack each end of ribbon inside cone on opposite sides.
Fill cone with dried flowers.

DOILY BASKET

Materials
5¼"- to 6"-diameter round
  embroidered cutwork doily
6" (¼"-wide) of matching braid or
  ribbon for handle
Thread to match
Vanishing fabric marker
Note: Adjust measurements to fit
  your doily, if necessary.

Instructions
1. With right sides facing, fold doily
in half. Referring to Diagram, use
marker to draw stitching lines, adjusting measurements, if necessary,
but maintaining shape.
2. Machine-stitch along each line,
using a long stitch. *Do not cut doily.*
Turn right side out and press.
3. For handle, tack each end of
braid or ribbon inside basket on opposite sides at center top.

Diagram: Shaping Doily Basket

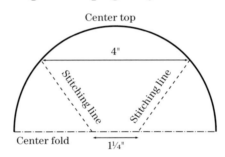

Center top

4"

Stitching line   Stitching line

Center fold   1¼"

MINI-CORNUCOPIA PIN OR MAGNET

Materials
¼ section of a small, round, damaged
  doily
Thread to match
Tiny safety pin (for pin) *or* adhesive-
  backed magnetic tape (for magnet)
4" (¼"-wide) of matching ribbon or
  braid for handle (optional)
Small dried flowers

Instructions
1. With right sides facing, fold doily
section in half, aligning straight
edges. Machine-stitch along straight
raw edges. Turn right side out, forming cone.
2. For optional handle, tack each
end of ribbon or braid inside cone on
opposite sides.
3. Sew pin or add narrow strip of
magnetic tape to back of cone. Fill
cone with dried flowers.

ROLLED MINI-CORNUCOPIA PIN OR MAGNET

Materials
3"- to 4"-diameter doily
12" (¹⁄₁₆"-wide) of contrasting satin
  ribbon
Thread to match
Tiny safety pin (for pin) *or* adhesive-
  backed magnetic tape (for magnet)
Small dried flowers

Instructions
Roll doily into cone shape and tack
along overlapped edges. Fill cone
with dried flowers. Tie ribbon in a
bow around cone. Sew pin or add
narrow strip of magnetic tape to
back of cone.

Memoo Board
Instructions are on page 50.

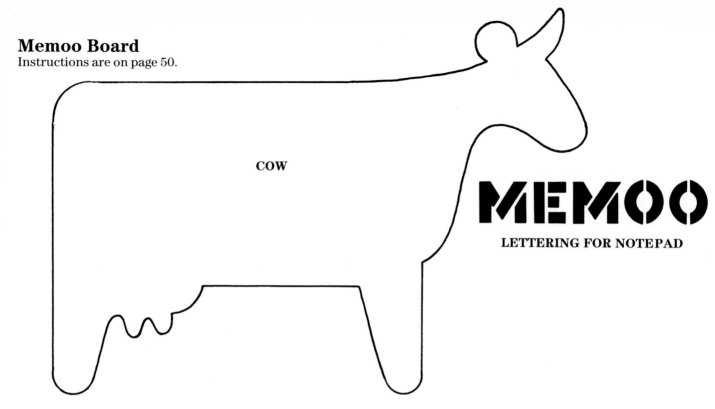

COW

MEMOO

LETTERING FOR NOTEPAD

Fabric Pinwheel
Instructions are on page 52.

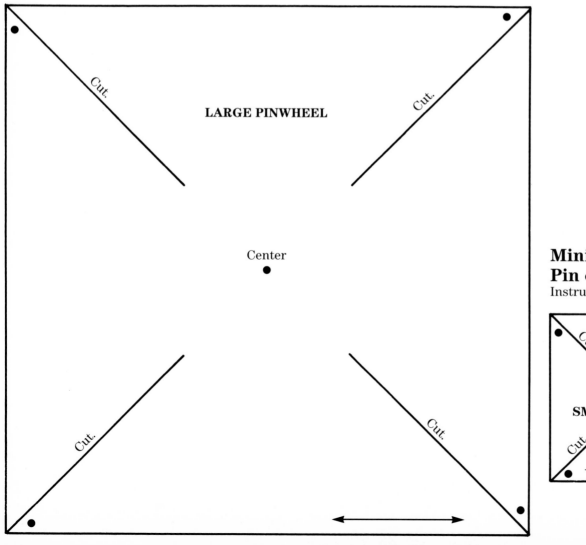

LARGE PINWHEEL

Cut.

Cut.

Cut.

Cut.

Center

Mini-Pinwheel
Pin or Magnet
Instructions are on page 53.

Cut.

Cut.

Center

SMALL PINWHEEL

Cut.

Cut.

Pinwheel Pot Holder

Instructions are on page 53.

Beach Ball

Instructions are on page 56.

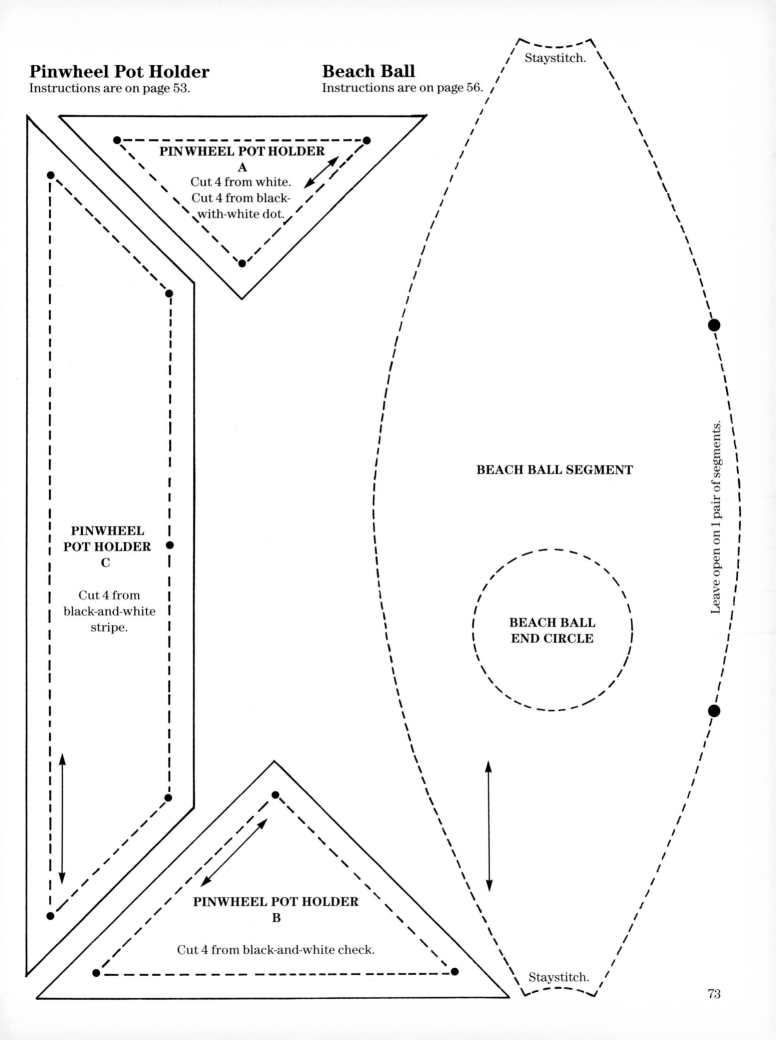

Staystitch.

**PINWHEEL POT HOLDER
A**

Cut 4 from white.
Cut 4 from black-
with-white dot.

**PINWHEEL
POT HOLDER
C**

Cut 4 from
black-and-white
stripe.

**PINWHEEL POT HOLDER
B**

Cut 4 from black-and-white check.

BEACH BALL SEGMENT

**BEACH BALL
END CIRCLE**

Leave open on 1 pair of segments.

Staystitch.

73

Match large black dot on 1 piece to white dot on other piece.

Fabric Softball
Instructions are on page 57.

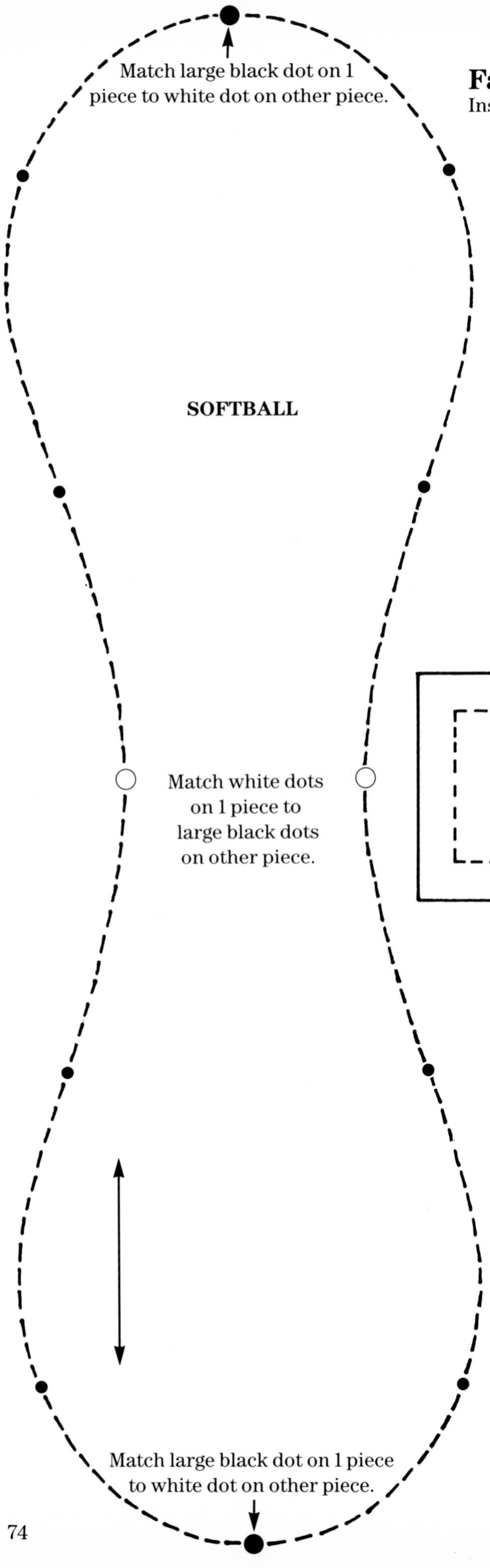

SOFTBALL

Match white dots on 1 piece to large black dots on other piece.

Bow Tie Mini-Pillow
Instructions are on page 58.

BOW TIE
A
Cut 1 from necktie silk.

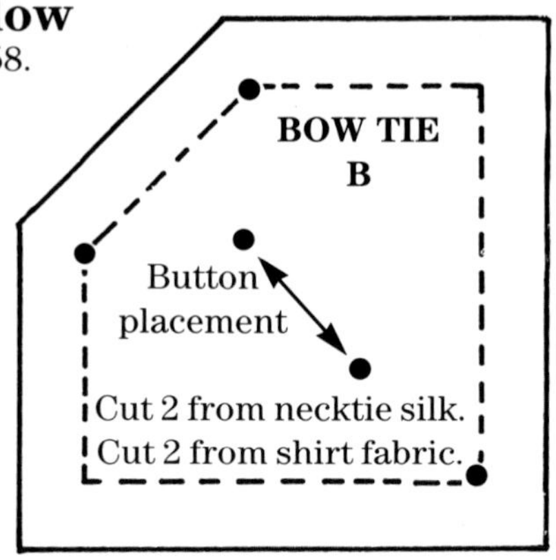

BOW TIE
B
Button placement
Cut 2 from necktie silk.
Cut 2 from shirt fabric.

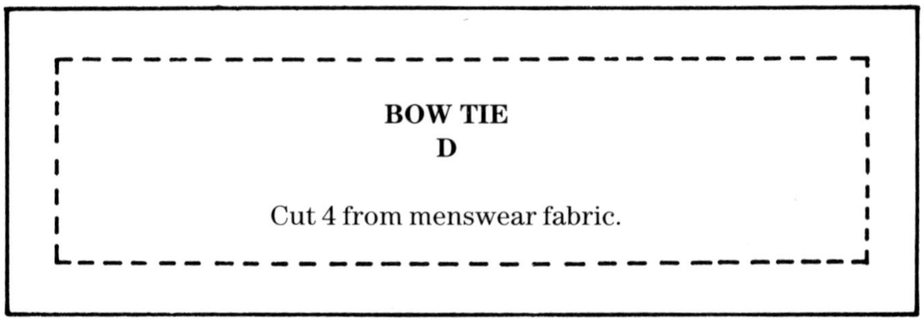

BOW TIE
D
Cut 4 from menswear fabric.

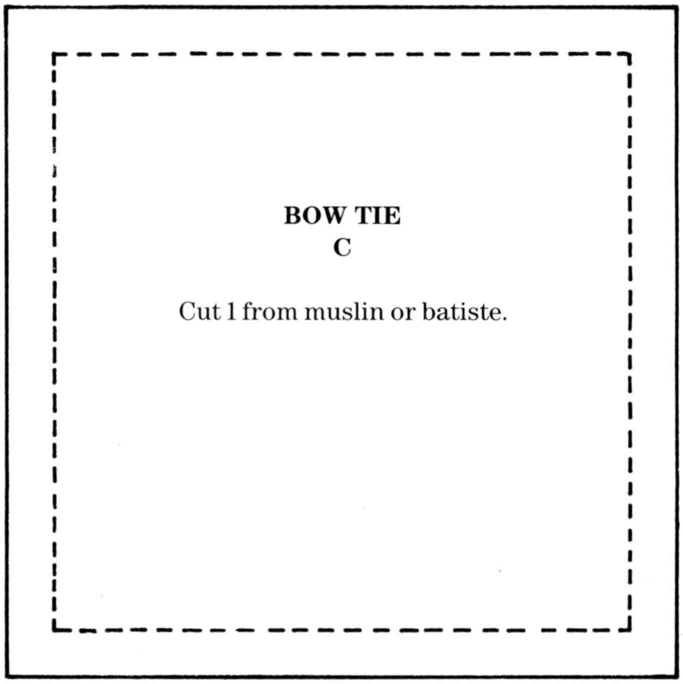

BOW TIE
C
Cut 1 from muslin or batiste.

Match large black dot on 1 piece to white dot on other piece.

Work Glove Bookends

Instructions are on page 58.

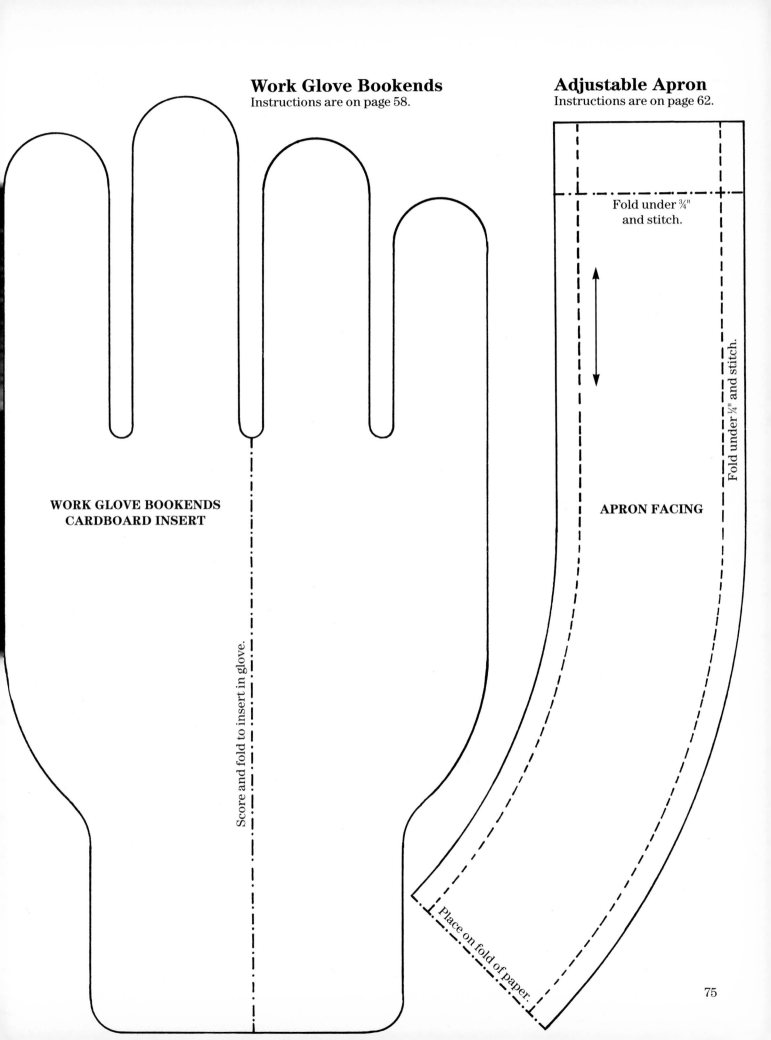

**WORK GLOVE BOOKENDS
CARDBOARD INSERT**

Score and fold to insert in glove.

Adjustable Apron

Instructions are on page 62.

Fold under ¾"
and stitch.

Fold under ¼" and stitch.

APRON FACING

Place on fold of paper.

75

Rickrack Flag or Appliqué

Instructions are on page 60.

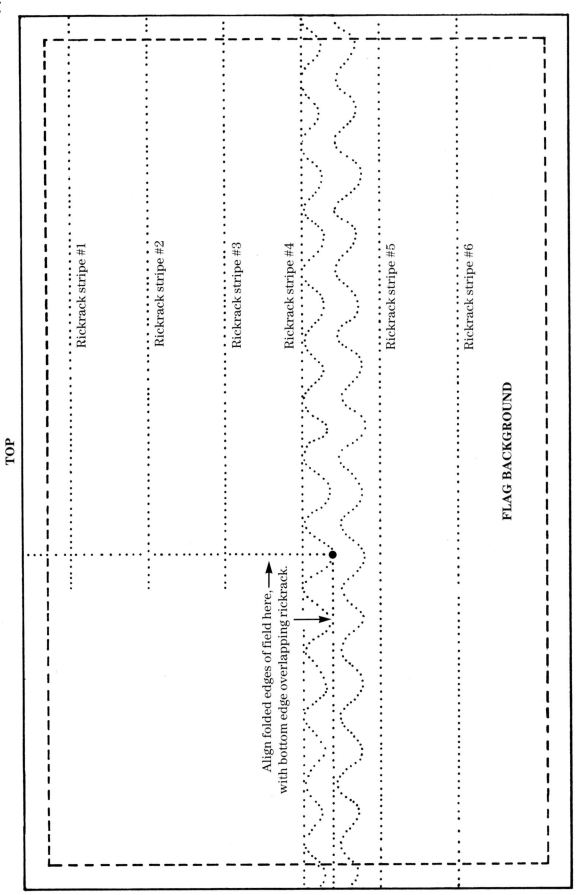

TOP

Rickrack stripe #1

Rickrack stripe #2

Rickrack stripe #3

Rickrack stripe #4

Rickrack stripe #5

Rickrack stripe #6

Align folded edges of field here,
with bottom edge overlapping rickrack.

FLAG BACKGROUND

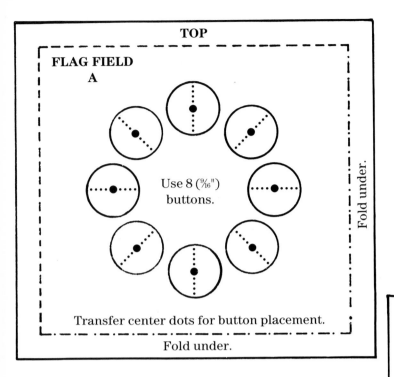

TOP

FLAG FIELD A

Use 8 (⁹⁄₁₆") buttons.

Transfer center dots for button placement.

Fold under.

Fold under.

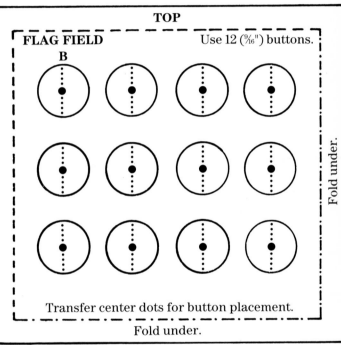

TOP

FLAG FIELD B

Use 12 (⁹⁄₁₆") buttons.

Transfer center dots for button placement.

Fold under.

Fold under.

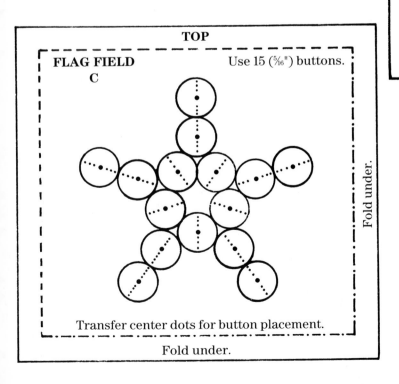

TOP

FLAG FIELD C

Use 15 (⁵⁄₁₆") buttons.

Transfer center dots for button placement.

Fold under.

Fold under.

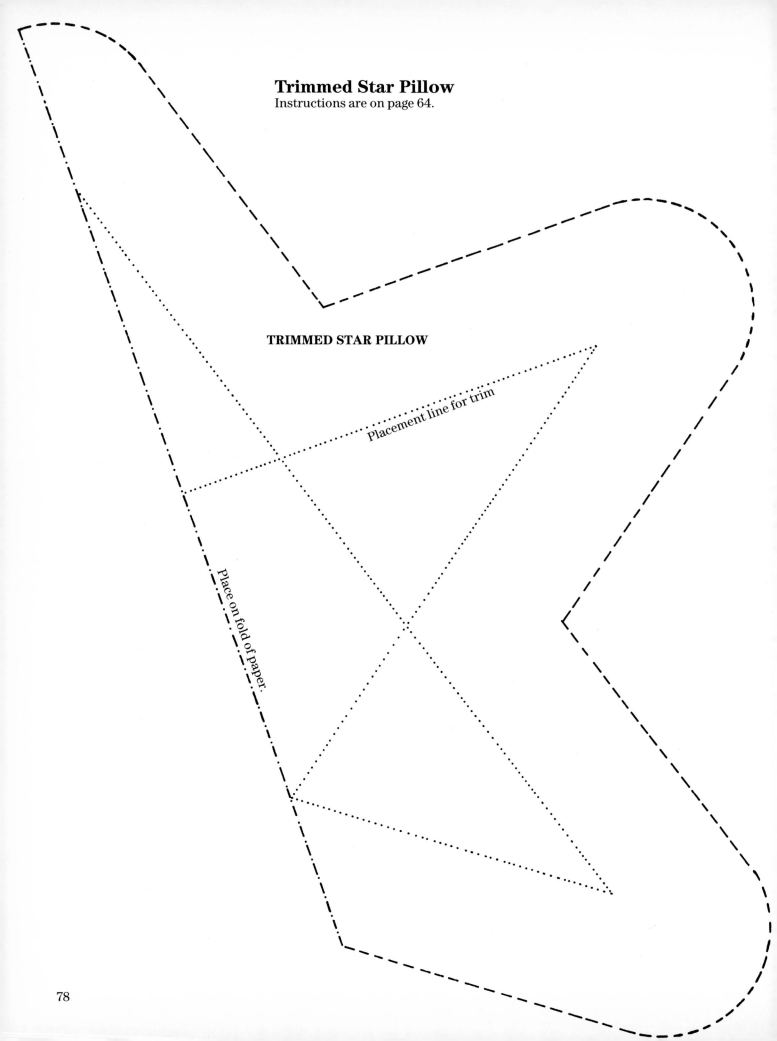

Trimmed Star Pillow
Instructions are on page 64.

TRIMMED STAR PILLOW

Placement line for trim

Place on fold of paper.

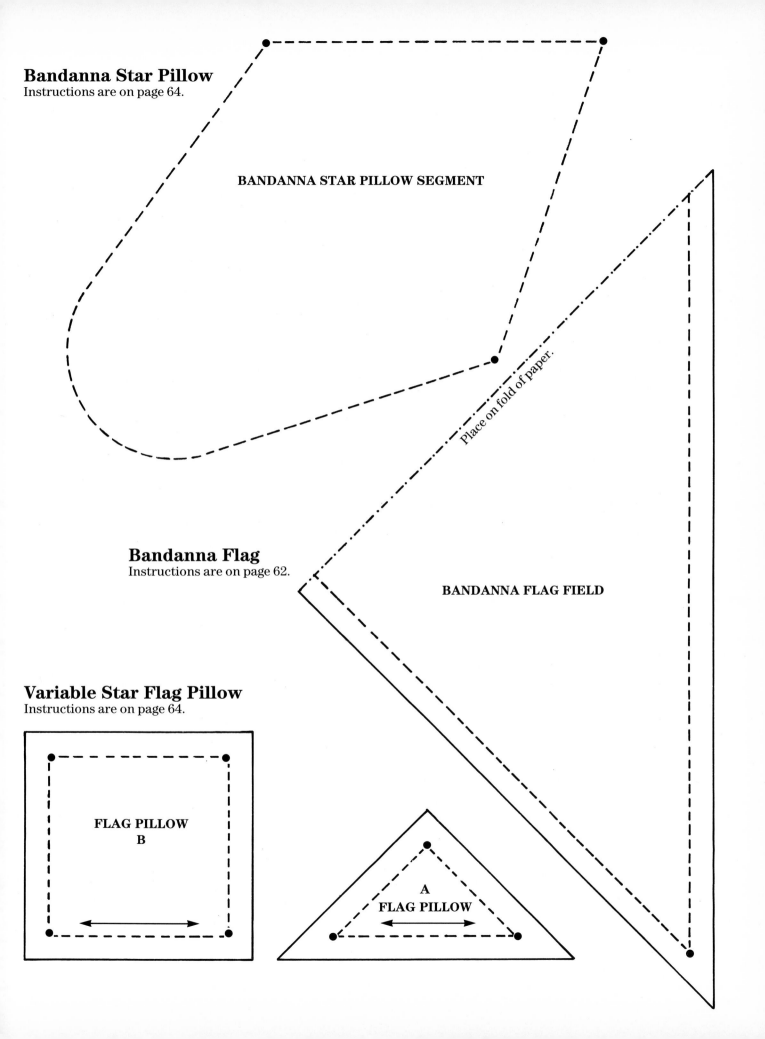

Bandanna Star Pillow
Instructions are on page 64.

BANDANNA STAR PILLOW SEGMENT

Place on fold of paper.

Bandanna Flag
Instructions are on page 62.

BANDANNA FLAG FIELD

Variable Star Flag Pillow
Instructions are on page 64.

FLAG PILLOW
B

A
FLAG PILLOW

COZY DAYS

Days are shorter and there's a chill in the air.

It's time to enjoy autumn's Cozy Days.

Gather the last herbs and flowers and hang them to dry.

Rake up a mountain of leaves and jump right in! Then step

inside to dream by the fire, snuggled down in a heartwarming

quilt. Filled to the brim with easy projects to celebrate

the season, this chapter is a harvest of ideas

for hearth and home.

HEART WARMERS

◆

This soft patchwork heart quilt is a perfect gift for someone who loves to snuggle up with a good book. It features hearts quickly pieced from strips of printed cotton and is decorated with old-fashioned yo-yos. The useful heart-shaped basket is fashioned from upholstery tape and a leftover candy box.

BURLAP HEART BASKET

Materials
2 yards (3½"-wide) of upholstery
   tape
3¼" x 32" piece of sturdy paper
Lid or bottom of 1-pound
   heart-shaped candy box
Craft glue

Instructions
  1. To fit paper to box, wrap paper around outside edge of box, overlapping ends ½"; trim, if necessary. Cut 1 piece of tape measuring ½" shorter than paper. Repeat to cut remaining piece of tape.
  2. Beginning ½" beyond crevice of heart and creasing at crevice, glue paper to box along sides; let dry. Repeat to glue 1 length of tape to paper along outside edge of box; trim tape at crevice. Repeat to glue remaining tape to paper along inside edge of box.

PATCHWORK HEART QUILT

Materials for (53" x 63") quilt
Pattern on page 104
3⅜ yards of small leaf print fabric
  for backing, borders, and
  yo-yos
1⅝ yards of plain or printed muslin
  for background
1⅝ yards of small floral print fabric
  for hearts and border
Thread to match
Embroidery floss to match backing
  fabric
54" x 64" piece of quilt batting
Graph paper
Extra-fine unwaxed dental floss

Instructions

1. Trace pattern pieces, transferring markings. To make pattern for setting blocks (E), draw 7½" x 8½" rectangle on graph paper. Make 4½"-diameter circle pattern for yo-yos. Cut out all patterns.

2. Trim ¼" from selvages on fabrics. Refer to Diagram 1 for cutting layouts.

Cut leaf print as follows: For backing, cut 2 (33" x 54") pieces. For borders, cut 2 (1½" x 61") strips, 2 (1½" x 54") strips, 2 (1½" x 52") strips, and 2 (1½" x 43¼") strips. From remaining leaf print, cut 17 (4½"-diameter) circles for yo-yos.

Cut muslin as follows: For patchwork, cut 3 (3½" x 54") strips, 1 (2½" x 54") strip, 36 Cs, 18 Ds, and 17 Es.

Cut floral print as follows: For border, cut 4 (5" x 52") strips; for patchwork, cut 4 (5" x 54") strips.

3. With right sides facing and long raw edges aligned, pin 1 (5" x 54") floral print strip and 1 (3½" x 54") muslin strip together; machine-stitch. Press seam open. Repeat to make 2 more strip-pieced bands.

On wrong side of 1 pieced band, align placement line of pattern A along seam line; trace, transferring dots, and cut out. Repeat, using all pieced bands, to cut 18 Unit As. Save scraps and set units aside.

4. To make Unit Bs, repeat Step 3, joining remaining 5" x 54" floral print strip to 2½" x 54" muslin strip, aligning placement line of pattern B along seam line, and cutting 14 units. From reserved scraps of pieced bands, cut 4 more Unit Bs.

Diagram 1: Cutting Layouts

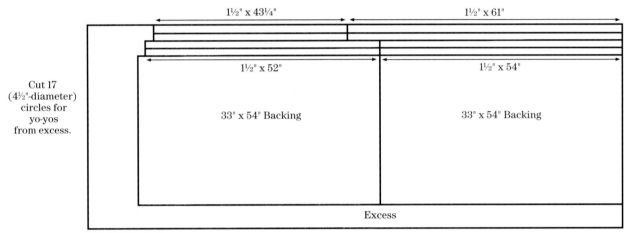

Cut 17 (4½"-diameter) circles for yo-yos from excess.

1½" x 43¼"   1½" x 61"

1½" x 52"   1½" x 54"

33" x 54" Backing   33" x 54" Backing

Excess

Leaf print for backing, borders, and yo-yos

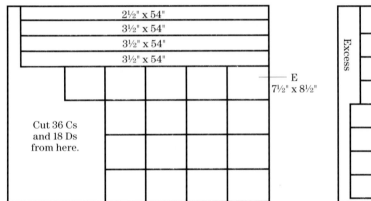

2½" x 54"
3½" x 54"
3½" x 54"
3½" x 54"

E
7½" x 8½"

Cut 36 Cs and 18 Ds from here.

Muslin for strip piecing and blocks

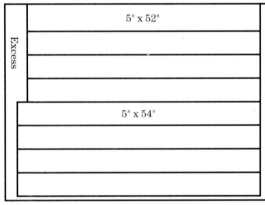

Excess

5" x 52"

5" x 54"

Floral print for strip piecing and border

5. Following Diagram 2, join pieces to make 1 (7½" x 8½") patchwork heart block. Repeat to make 18 blocks. Alternating placement of patchwork blocks and muslin Es, join 5 blocks to make a horizontal row. Repeat to make 7 rows. Join rows together (see photo).

Diagram 2:
Assembling Patchwork Block

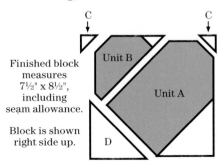

C   C

Unit B

Unit A

Finished block measures 7½" x 8½", including seam allowance.

Block is shown right side up.

D

6. To add borders, with right sides facing and raw edges aligned, pin 1 (1½" x 52") leaf print strip to each side of quilt top; machine-stitch. Trim any excess. Repeat to join 1½" x 43¼" leaf print strips to top and bottom of quilt top.

In same manner, join 5" x 52" floral print strips to sides, top, and bottom of quilt top. For final border, join 1 (1½" x 61") leaf print strip to each side; then join 1½" x 54" leaf print strips to top and bottom.

7. For backing, with right sides facing and raw edges aligned, machine-stitch backing pieces together along 1 long edge. Press seam open. Trim backing to match size of quilt top.

Stack batting; backing (right side up); and quilt top (right side down). Pin all layers together. Machine-stitch edges together, leaving 6" opening for turning. Trim excess batting; turn and slipstitch opening closed.

Flatten edges. Pin; then securely baste layers together. Machine-stitch in-the-ditch along all border seams.

8. To make 1 yo-yo, turn under ¼" around edge of 1 circle. Thread needle with dental floss; run gathering stitches through both layers of folded edge. Pull floss tightly to gather and tie off. Flatten yo-yo, centering opening; distribute gathers evenly. Repeat to make 17 yo-yos.

Tack 1 yo-yo to center of each muslin E, stitching through top layer of quilt only. Thread a needle with 6 strands of embroidery floss and take 1 stitch through center of yo-yo from back of quilt, leaving 3"-long tails. Knot tails together with a double knot and trim tails as desired.

WARM COZIES

◆

Chase away an autumn chill with a cup of fragrant tea. Your own quilted cozy keeps the pot warm. For an extra caring touch, you can add a silver star sticker to each tea bag.

And you can create homey gifts like the cookie cutter dolls, soft fabric turtles, or a pocket-size checkers game made from woven ribbons.

TEA COZY

Materials

Pattern on pages 105–106
⅓ yard of blue quilted fabric for cozy
⅓ yard of white quilted fabric for lining
2¼ yards of white corded piping
Thread to match
1" acrylic pom-pom
Zipper foot for sewing machine

Instructions

1. Trace pattern pieces on folded paper, transferring markings. Cut out.

2. Cut pieces for cozy and lining as indicated on pattern. Transfer markings; on right side of each cozy side piece, use basting stitches to mark placement of spout and handle on alternate edges. For handles, cut 2 (1½" x 12") strips from crosswise grain of blue quilted fabric.

3. With right sides facing and raw edges aligned, pin cozy side pieces together; stitch each straight edge, forming center front and center back seams. Slipstitch seam allowances in place, stitching through 1 layer only; turn cozy side unit right side out.

Starting at center back on bottom curved edge and aligning raw edges, baste piping to right side of cozy side unit. Overlap piping at center back, trim excess, and clip seam allowance. Repeat to baste piping around top curved edge. Turn unit to wrong side. Set aside cozy side unit and remaining piping.

4. For cozy lid, with right sides facing and straight raw edges aligned, machine-stitch center back seam. Slipstitch each seam allowance in place, stitching through 1 layer only. With right sides facing, center back seams aligned, and dots matching, place lid inside cozy side unit; baste. Machine-stitch lid and cozy side unit together. Clip seam allowance and turn.

5. On lining pieces, staystitch all curved edges. Repeat Step 3 to assemble lining side unit, omitting piping. With right sides facing and raw edges and seams aligned, pin cozy and lining together along bottom curved edge. Using zipper foot, machine-stitch; turn right side out through opening at top of lining. Pin along lower edge to secure layers. Baste lining and cozy seam allowances together around top edge.

6. For lining lid, stitch center back seam and slipstitch seam allowance as described in Step 4. Turn under ¼" around outer edge and baste. Slipstitch lid to lining, covering top basted raw edges of lining and cozy.

7. Staystitch long curved edge of cozy spout and lining spout pieces. With right sides facing and raw edges aligned, pin cozy spout and lining spout together along short curved edge; machine-stitch. Trim seam allowance to ⅛" and clip curves. Open unit and fold in half lengthwise, with right sides facing and center seam matching (see Diagram).

Machine-stitch straight edges together, pivoting at center seam; slipstitch seam allowances in place, stitching through 1 layer only. On each curved edge, turn under ¼" to wrong side and baste. Turn; pin and slipstitch basted edges together. Pin spout in place and slipstitch to tea cozy center front.

Diagram: Stitching Spout

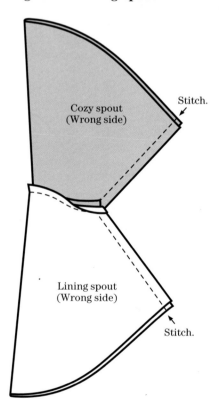

Cozy spout
(Wrong side)

Stitch.

Lining spout
(Wrong side)

Stitch.

8. Measure and pin 1 length cut from remaining piping to each long edge of 1 handle strip, aligning raw edges. On remaining handle strip, turn under ¼" on 1 long edge and baste. With right sides facing and raw edges aligned, pin handle strips together along long unhemmed edge; using zipper foot, machine-stitch. Open and refold with wrong sides facing. Slipstitch along remaining long edge. Fold 1 short end ½" to front and 1 short end ½" to back. Referring to photo and aligning with basting stitches, pin each end of handle in place; slipstitch bottom edge of each end to cozy and 1½" along each side to conceal cut ends. Tack pom-pom to center top of lid.

WOVEN RIBBON CHECKERS GAME

Materials
6" x 12" piece of black felt
1⅜ yards (⅝"-wide) of red grosgrain ribbon
1⅜ yards (⅝"-wide) of black grosgrain ribbon
1½ yards (⅜"-wide) of black grosgrain ribbon
10" (⅛"-wide) of black grosgrain ribbon
10" (⅛"-wide) of red grosgrain ribbon
Thread to match
White pencil
Transparent tape
12 (½") red buttons
12 (½") black buttons
½" red button and ½" black button for ribbon ties (optional)

Instructions
1. Referring to Diagram 1 for measurements, use white pencil to mark felt.

2. Cut 8 (5¾") lengths each from ⅝"-wide red ribbon and ⅝"-wide black ribbon. From ⅜"-wide black ribbon, cut 4 (5¾") lengths; set aside remainder.

3. Referring to Diagram 2, position 8 lengths of red ribbon on felt, securing cut ends with tape. (Ribbon edges must butt together so that no black felt shows through.) Baste ribbons in place along width; remove tape.

4. Place 1 length of ⅜"-wide black ribbon on top basted ends of red ribbons, aligning black ribbon with marked lines on felt; machine-stitch along each edge of black ribbon.

5. Beginning at top left corner, weave 1 length of ⅝"-wide black ribbon under and over red ribbons repeatedly. Continue weaving with remaining lengths of ⅝"-wide black ribbon, butting long edges closely together and securing cut ends with tape. Baste ribbons in place along sides and bottom of checkerboard area; remove tape.

6. Place 1 length of ⅜"-wide black ribbon on bottom basted ends of red ribbons; machine-stitch along each edge of black ribbon. Along top and bottom, whipstitch edge of each section of woven black ribbon to edge of ⅜"-wide ribbon.

Machine-stitch 1 length of ⅜"-wide black ribbon along each pocket edge of felt piece.

7. From remaining ⅜"-wide black ribbon, cut 2 (13") lengths. Place 1 length along each long edge of felt; fold over ½" on each end and tack in place. Taking care not to catch edges of woven red ribbons in seams, machine-stitch along each edge.

To make pockets, fold felt to back along ribbons at top and bottom of checkerboard. Baste each folded pocket in place. To secure pockets, topstitch along each edge of ribbons surrounding checkerboard.

8. For ties, tack ⅛"-wide red ribbon to center of 1 side of checkerboard and ⅛"-wide black ribbon to opposite side (see photo). If desired, tie matching color button to end of each ribbon.

Insert 12 red buttons in 1 pocket and 12 black buttons in the other pocket; fold checkerboard at center and tie ribbon ties in a bow.

Diagram 1: Marking Felt

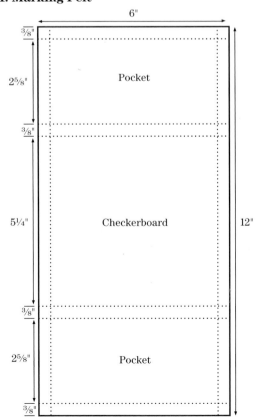

Diagram 2: Ribbon Placement

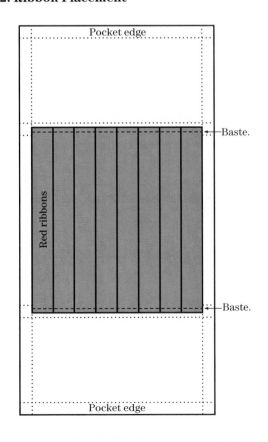

BUTTON TURTLE

Materials for one large turtle

Pattern on page 108
2 (6½") squares of fabric for body
6½" square of contrasting or
  coordinating fabric for yo-yo
  shell
Thread to match
Embroidery floss: darker shade of
  body fabric color
Polyester stuffing
Small dowel or crochet hook
Vanishing fabric marker
Extra-fine unwaxed dental floss
1⅛" or larger button for shell

Instructions

1. Trace pattern pieces on folded paper, transferring markings. Cut out.

2. With right sides facing and raw edges aligned, baste squares of body fabric together. On 1 side, trace 1 body pattern. *Do not cut out yet.* Stitch by hand or machine completely around shape. Trim seam allowance to ⅛"; clip curves.

Carefully make slit through 1 layer of fabric as indicated on pattern. Use dowel or crochet hook to push head and legs inside body and turn right side out through slit. Pull tail out using a needle or pin. Flatten turtle and transfer markings, including shell line on both sides of body and eye placement on slit side of body.

3. Stuff turtle firmly. Whipstitch slit closed. (Yo-yo shell will cover stitching.) Make running stitches along marked shell line, stitching through all layers.

4. Using 2 strands of embroidery floss, satin-stitch eyes. For claws, make straight stitches where indicated on pattern, from bottom of foot to top, wrapping thread tightly around front edge of foot. Tie off securely.

5. To make yo-yo shell, trace pattern on right side of fabric. Cut out, adding ¼" seam allowance. Turn under ¼" around edge. With needle threaded with dental floss, run gathering stitches through both layers on folded edge. Pull floss tightly to gather and tie off. Flatten yo-yo, centering opening; distribute gathers evenly.

Place shell on turtle, aligning edge of yo-yo with running stitches at neck and tail. Slipstitch underside of yo-yo shell to body, allowing top of yo-yo to extend beyond sides of body. Stitch button to center of yo-yo. Fold head up and legs down along shell line.

TURTLE BABY

Materials for one small turtle

Pattern on page 108
2 (3½") squares of fabric for body
3½" square of contrasting or
  coordinating fabric for yo-yo
  shell (optional)
Thread to match
Embroidery floss: darker shade of
  body fabric color
Polyester stuffing
Bamboo skewer or crochet hook
Vanishing fabric marker
Extra-fine unwaxed dental floss
  (optional)
1⅜" button for shell *or* ½" button for
  optional yo-yo shell

Instructions

1. To make small turtle, refer to Steps 1–4 of Button Turtle, making French knots for eyes.

2. For yo-yo shell, refer to Step 5 of Button Turtle. For button shell, omit yo-yo and stitch large button to center of turtle body, using embroidery floss.

COUNTRY ACCENT

These tiny nosegays are reminiscent of roadside market stands selling stacks of pumpkins, bushels of apples, and autumn bouquets wrapped in newspaper. They can decorate an individual place setting, be worn as a pin, or serve as a pretty kitchen magnet.

Gather a bunch of small dried flowers with stems about two inches long. Place them diagonally on a 4½"-square piece of newspaper from the classified section. Wrap the newspaper around the flowers loosely and then gather it closely around the stems. Tie string or jute around the newspaper. On the back of the bouquet, secure the ends of the newspaper with tape and glue on a pin fastener or a small magnet.

HAPPY HALLOWEEN

◆

This old house with its tree full of spooky spiders gives a festive welcome to trick-or-treaters. Use the same pattern to make a handy reusable bag for collecting Halloween treats or turn the block into a colorful pot holder.

You'll also find a friendly Halloween cat with its own mask and a paper "batsket" to fill with a generous handful of goodies.

HAUNTED HOUSE WELCOME SIGN OR TRICK-OR-TREAT BAG

Materials
Pattern on page 109
5" x 8" piece of purple fabric
8½" square of black fabric
2½" x 3½" scrap of yellow fabric
3 (8") squares of fabric for lining/backing
3¾" (⅛"-wide) of black grosgrain ribbon
6" (⅛"-wide) of orange grosgrain ribbon
50" (½"-wide) of black double-fold bias tape
Thread to match
Transparent nylon thread
2 (8") squares of quilt batting
White pencil
Vanishing fabric marker
¾" x 1⅝" scrap of sturdy white paper
Black fine-point marker
⅛" paper punch
Dry twigs
Small black plastic spiders

Diagram: Block Assembly

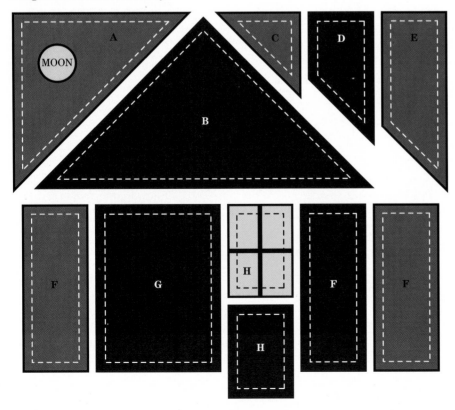

Instructions

1. Trace pattern pieces, transferring markings. Cut out.

2. Using white pencil to mark dark fabrics and fabric marker to mark light fabrics, trace patterns at least ½" apart on wrong side of fabrics. Adding ¼" seam allowances, cut out pieces as indicated on pattern, transferring markings. On right side of A, trace moon placement line. On right side of yellow H, trace ribbon placement lines.

3. Clip and press under seam allowance around moon. Align moon with marked placement line on A and appliqué in place.

From black ribbon, cut 1 (2¼"-long) piece and 1 (1½"-long) piece. Aligning with corresponding marked placement lines on yellow H, stitch pieces in place by hand or machine.

4. Referring to Diagram, assemble pieced block. Press all seams toward darker fabric.

5. Stack backing (right side down); batting; and house block (centered and right side up). Batting and backing will extend ¼" beyond block. Baste layers together. Bind top edge only with bias tape.

6. To make bag back, stack 1 lining/backing piece (right side down); batting; and remaining lining/backing piece (right side up). Baste layers together and bind 1 edge with bias tape.

7. With 2 lining/backing sides facing and bound edges aligned, baste bag front and bag back together along unbound edges. Bind basted bottom edges together with bias tape. With remaining bias tape, bind 1 side of bag, leaving 18½" free at top for handle, and then continue binding other side of bag. Slipstitch open edges of handle together.

8. For Welcome Sign, trace letters on white paper with black marker. Punch holes as indicated on pattern. Thread orange ribbon through holes and knot each end. Referring to photo, tack center of ribbon to bottom of window. Fill bag with twigs. To add spiders, thread needle with nylon thread and stitch through bottom of 1 spider; knot thread. Tie other end of thread to twig. Repeat to add remaining spiders.

For Trick-or-Treat Bag, omit twigs and spiders.

HAUNTED HOUSE POT HOLDER

Materials

Pattern on page 109
5" x 8" piece of purple fabric
8½" square of black fabric
2½" x 3½" scrap of yellow fabric
8" square of fabric for backing
9¼" (⅛"-wide) of black grosgrain
    ribbon
36" (½"-wide) of black double-fold
    bias tape
Thread to match
8" square of extra-thick quilt
    batting
White pencil
Vanishing fabric marker

Instructions

To assemble pot holder, follow Steps 1–5 of Haunted House Welcome Sign or Trick-or-Treat Bag, on page 94, binding all edges with bias tape.

If hanger loop is desired, fold remaining black ribbon in half to form loop; tack to back of pot holder at center top.

HALLOWEEN CAT

Materials

Pattern on pages 110–111
10" x 36" piece of tightly woven print
    fabric
26½" (⅜"-wide) of orange grosgrain
    ribbon
Thread to match
Black embroidery floss for eyes *or* 2
    (¼") short-shank black buttons
Polyester stuffing

Instructions

Note: For constructing cat, use small machine stitches, backstitching at beginning and ending of all seams; trim all seams to ⅛" and clip all curves.

1. Trace pattern pieces, transferring markings. Cut out.

2. Placing patterns at least ½" apart on wrong side of fabric and adding ¼" seam allowances, trace and cut out all pieces except ears; transfer markings. Set aside scraps. On right side of fabric, use basting stitches to mark placement lines for eyes and ears on head side and head top pieces.

From remaining scraps, cut 2 (3") squares. With right sides facing and raw edges aligned, fold 1 square in half diagonally. Referring to Diagram, Figure A, align ear pattern on fold and trace. Machine-stitch along marked line, leaving open between dots. Cut out, adding ⅛" seam allowance. Clip curves and turn. Slipstitch opening closed. Repeat for remaining ear. Set aside.

3. With right sides facing and raw edges aligned, pin body side pieces together along top edge, from top of neck to rear dot; machine-stitch.

With right sides facing and raw edges aligned, pin underbody pieces together along center tummy seam, from top of neck to rear dot; then machine-stitch.

With right sides facing and raw edges aligned, pin underbody unit to body side unit from rear dot, around legs, and up to bottom of neck; machine-stitch. Turn right side out. By hand, use doubled thread to staystitch around neckline. Stuff body firmly, shaping as you work.

4. With right sides facing and raw edges aligned, pin head side pieces

Decked out in colors of the season and a Cat-o'-lantern Mask, these Halloween Cats will be an added treat to the holiday. Bright candy corn fills the Halloween "Batsket" (center) that's easily made from black art paper.

together along chin seam line. Machine-stitch; then clip curve. Along each remaining curved edge, clip seam allowances.

On head top piece, stitch dart. With right sides facing, raw edges aligned, and dots matching at nose, pin and baste head side unit to head top. Beginning at X, machine-stitch together, easing in fullness; pivot at nose and continue stitching to remaining X. By hand, use doubled thread to staystitch around neckline. Stuff head firmly. Turn neckline seam allowance under and baste.

5. Pin head to body, matching seams. By hand, use doubled thread to slipstitch head to body. Softly fold each ear as shown in Figure B. Slipstitch bottom edge of each ear to

head along basted placement line (see Figure C). If using buttons for eyes, stitch each in place securely. To embroider eyes, use 2 strands of floss to satin-stitch $\frac{1}{4}$" circles at placement markings. Cut ends of ribbon diagonally and tie in a bow around neck of cat.

Diagram: Making Ear

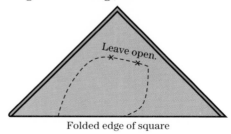

Leave open.

Folded edge of square

Figure A

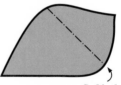

Figure B

Softly fold.

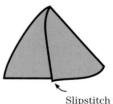

Figure C

Slipstitch this edge to head.

CAT-O'-LANTERN MASK

Materials
Pattern on page 111
4" square of orange paper
Craft knife
⅛" paper punch
24" jute or twine

Instructions
1. Trace pattern, transferring markings. Cut out.
2. Holding pattern in place with paper clips, trace onto orange paper. On protected surface, cut out mask and facial features. Punch out holes. Cut jute or twine in half. Thread 1 piece through each hole in mask and knot. Place mask on Halloween Cat and tie ends together.

HALLOWEEN "BATSKET"

Materials
Pattern on page 112
5" x 11" piece of sturdy black art paper
1" square of purple paper
Craft knife
White glue
⅛" paper punch

Instructions
1. Trace pattern pieces, transferring markings. Cut out.
2. Trace handle/base strip pattern along length of black paper. Cut out. On remaining paper, trace bat pattern 2 times and cut out. Score all tabs and fold lines as indicated on patterns; fold.
3. Glue folded tab at 1 end of handle/base strip to opposite end of strip (see Diagram). Let dry.
4. Apply glue to tabs on 1 bat. Glue bottom tabs to inside of handle/base strip at center bottom. Glue wing tabs to inside of handle/base strip on each side, just above strip folds.

Gently separate bat and handle/base strip enough to apply glue to side tabs on handle/base strip. Press pieces together; let dry. Repeat with remaining bat.

5. Punch 4 circles from purple paper. Clip off top of each circle to make eye shape shown on pattern. Glue 2 eyes in place on each side.

**Diagram:
Assembling Handle/Base Strip**

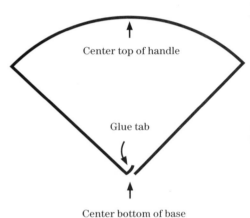

Center top of handle

Glue tab

Center bottom of base

COUNTRY ACCENT

Glistening rows of canning jars filled with the garden's harvest are a staple in a country pantry. But you can "put up" even more than you produce! Fill a clean pint or quart jar with brightly colored spools of thread, tomato pincushions, buttons, pencils, or other small items. Use a piece of solid-colored paper to cover the flat portion of a two-piece lid and top it off with a self-sticking star, if you like. Wrap it all up with a matching ribbon or add a bright yellow tape-measure bow.

THANKSGIVING TREATS

◆

The colors of maple leaves on this wreath and the matching coasters glow throughout the autumn and welcome the celebration of Thanksgiving Day. Decorate your table with paper pumpkins filled with savory nuts and use a cookie cutter to make an easy country-style ornament.

MAPLE LEAF WREATH

Materials
Pattern on page 112
1 (4½" x 6") piece each of solid fabrics for leaves: gold, orange, red-orange, bright red, maroon, brown
8" x 24" piece of green print fabric for leaves background
4½" x 20" piece of coordinating print fabric for setting triangles
16" square of fabric for backing
17" (⅛"-wide) of brown grosgrain ribbon for stems
2¼ yards (¼"-wide) of brown double-fold bias tape

Thread to match
Brown quilting thread
Embroidery floss to match backing
16" square of thin quilt batting
Polyester stuffing
Blunt pencil or crochet hook
Vanishing fabric marker or white pencil
Craft glue
10" embroidery hoop (1 ring)

Instructions
1. Trace pattern pieces, transferring markings and piercing matching dots with large needle. Cut out.

2. Trace 3 As and 4 Bs on wrong side of 1 fabric for 1 leaf, transferring dots; cut out. Repeat with remaining leaves fabrics.

On wrong side of leaves background fabric, trace 12 As and 24 Bs, transferring dots; cut out. On right side of 6 background As, mark diagonally from corner to corner for stem placement line.

On wrong side of coordinating fabric, trace 6 Cs for setting triangles, transferring dots. From ribbon, cut 6 (2¾") strips.

3. Glue 1 ribbon strip to each marked A along placement line. Machine-stitch long edges of each strip. Referring to Diagram 1, assemble 1 leaf block. (Press all seams as you work.)

Repeat with remaining As and Bs to complete 6 blocks.

4. On flat surface, arrange leaf blocks and Cs as shown in Diagram 2, *with straight grain of each C along outside edge of wreath.* Stitching between marked dots and backstitching at beginning and end of each seam, join patchwork blocks and Cs. Press all seams between units in same direction.

Referring to Diagram 3, lightly mark quilting lines, using fabric marker or white pencil. Center wreath (right side up) on batting and pin together. *Do not trim batting yet.* Quilt by hand along marked lines.

5. With wrong sides facing, center quilted wreath top on backing fabric. Machine-stitch around center of wreath. Backstitching at outside edge and stitching toward center, begin topstitching each triangle in-the-ditch along 1 side seam; pivot at tip and continue stitching to outside edge. Backstitch. (Leave outside edge of each triangle and each leaf block open for stuffing.) Trim excess batting and backing.

Stuff each leaf block, using a blunt pencil or crochet hook to push batting into all corners; then stuff triangles. Flatten wreath as you work.

6. Baste layers together ⅜" from raw outside edge. Machine-stitch ¼" from outside edge. Remove basting and trim 1/16" from seam. (Clip seam allowances, if necessary, to be sure that wreath lies flat.) Bind edges with bias tape, making a tiny pleat at each inside corner.

With floss, tack embroidery hoop to back of wreath in center of each square and triangle.

**Diagram 1:
Assembling Leaf Block**

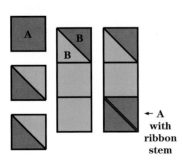

← A with ribbon stem

Diagram 2: Arranging Wreath

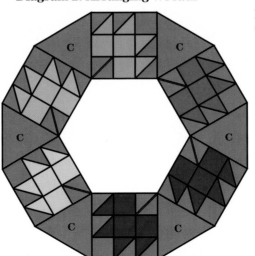

**Diagram 3:
Quilting Leaf Block**

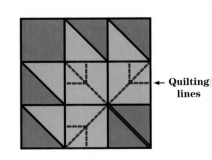

← Quilting lines

Stitch the Maple Leaf Wreath (top) in warm country colors and cut colorful art paper into a Pumpkin Nut Cup (left). Assemble the Cookie Cutter Animal Ornament (right) with materials found around the house: wooden buttons, jute, a wooden bead, and ribbon.

MAPLE LEAF COASTERS

Materials for one coaster
Pattern on page 112
4½" x 6" scrap of print fabric for leaf
4½" square of print fabric for leaf
   background
4½" square of coordinating terry
   cloth for backing
2¾" (⅛"-wide) of brown or green
   grosgrain ribbon for stem
18" (¼"-wide) of coordinating
   double-fold bias tape
Thread to match
Craft glue

Instructions
1. Trace pattern pieces, transferring markings and piercing matching dots with large needle. Cut out.
2. On wrong side of leaf fabric, trace 3 As and 4 Bs, transferring dots. Cut out. On wrong side of background fabric, trace 2 As and 4 Bs. On right side of 1 background A, mark diagonally from corner to corner for stem placement line.
3. Refer to Step 3 of Maple Leaf Wreath, on page 100, to add stem and assemble 1 leaf block. Use a small tumbler as a guide to mark rounded edges at each corner. Trim excess.
4. Place leaf block (right side up) on terry cloth and baste together. Machine-stitch layers together; trim excess terry cloth. Bind edges with bias tape.

*A*utumn *prints and the leaf block pattern from the Maple Leaf Wreath, on page 100, create Maple Leaf Coasters. Stitch them with fabrics used in the wreath for a coordinated look.*

COOKIE CUTTER ANIMAL ORNAMENT

Materials
3"- to 3½"-high animal-shaped cookie
   cutter
10" (¼"-wide) of ribbon
4 (⅞") coordinating buttons *or* 4
   bobbins
7" of jute *or* silver thread
10-mm wooden bead *or* small jingle
   bell
Craft glue

Instructions
Glue 2 buttons or bobbins along bottom edge on each side of animal cookie cutter. Tie ribbon in bow around animal's neck; trim excess, if necessary.

For decorative handle, glue 1 end of jute or silver thread under bottom front of cookie cutter. Thread other end through bead or jingle bell and tie in knot.

*M*etal bobbins, silver thread, a jingle bell, and gingham ribbon make the Cookie Cutter Animal Ornament shine.*

PUMPKIN NUT CUP

Materials
Pattern on page 113
7" square of orange art paper
4¼" square of green art paper
Craft knife
Masking tape
White glue
⅛" paper punch
2 (⅜"-long) brad paper fasteners for handle (optional)

Instructions
1. Trace pattern pieces, transferring markings. Cut out.

2. Tape pumpkin pattern onto orange paper, trace around shape, and transfer markings. Lightly score horizontal fold lines. Slit paper vertically at ⅜" intervals as indicated on pattern.

From remaining orange scrap, cut out base; lightly score along broken lines and fold. Set aside.

From green paper, cut stem; also cut optional handle, if desired. If adding handle, punch holes as indicated on stem and handle patterns.

3. Referring to Diagram, Figure A, fold core area and Tab A. Glue Tab A inside of core area along opposite side. Let dry.

Referring to Figure B, curl pumpkin slits; glue Tab B to inside of core area along opposite side. Hold pieces in place until dry.

4. Referring to pattern, form stem piece into a cylinder by gluing overlap area to inside of opposite side. Beginning at bottom of core area, gently insert stem into core area; carefully glue stem piece to core area between paper layers at open bottom of pumpkin.

5. On pumpkin base, lightly score and fold tabs as indicated on pattern. Apply small amount of glue to all tabs. Center base on open bottom and glue tabs to pumpkin slits.

If desired, attach handle to stem with brad fasteners.

Diagram: Making Pumpkin

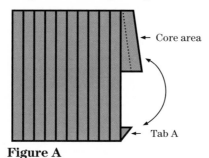

Figure A

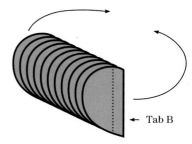

Figure B

COUNTRY ACCENT

Save colorful containers from the supermarket to make pretty vases. Fill the tins or boxes with generous bunches of dried flowers. Or, to hold fresh flowers, insert small glass or plastic containers inside the tins to hold water.

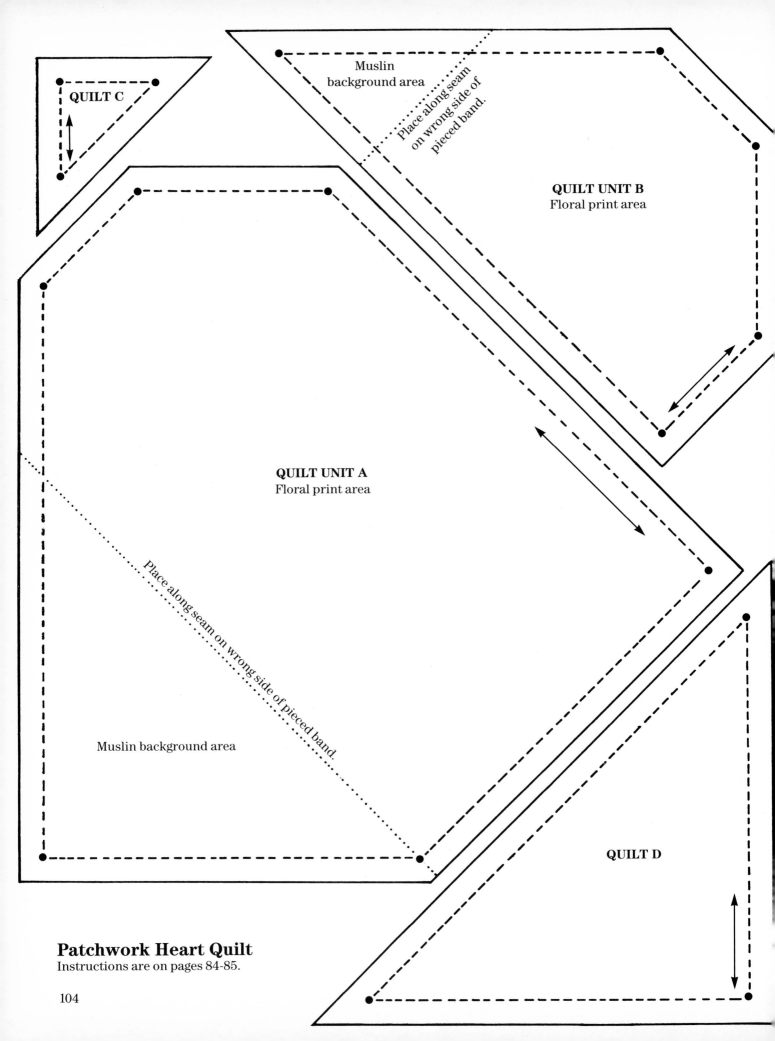

QUILT C

Muslin
background area

Place along seam
on wrong side of
pieced band.

QUILT UNIT B
Floral print area

QUILT UNIT A
Floral print area

Place along seam on wrong side of pieced band.

Muslin background area

QUILT D

Patchwork Heart Quilt
Instructions are on pages 84-85.

104

Tea Cozy

Instructions are on pages 86-87.

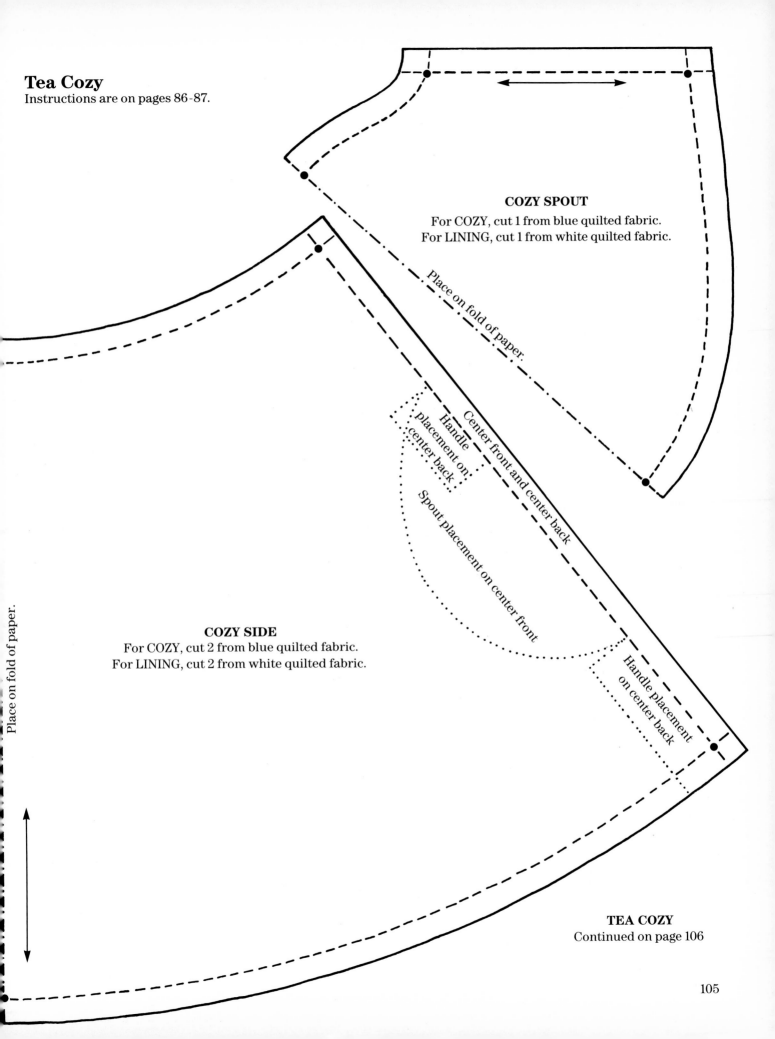

COZY SPOUT

For COZY, cut 1 from blue quilted fabric.
For LINING, cut 1 from white quilted fabric.

Place on fold of paper.

Center front and center back

Handle placement on center back

Spout placement on center front

Handle placement on center back

COZY SIDE

For COZY, cut 2 from blue quilted fabric.
For LINING, cut 2 from white quilted fabric.

Place on fold of paper.

TEA COZY
Continued on page 106

105

Place on fold of paper.

Center back

COZY LID
For COZY, cut 1 from blue quilted fabric.
For LINING, cut 1 from white quilted fabric.

Cookie Cutter Baby

Instructions are on page 88.

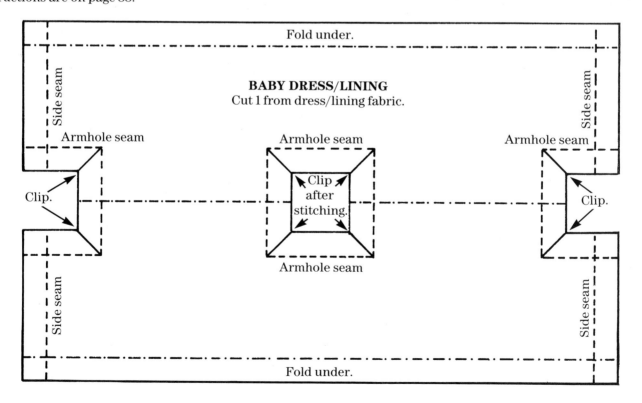

Fold under.

Side seam

Side seam

BABY DRESS/LINING
Cut 1 from dress/lining fabric.

Armhole seam

Armhole seam

Armhole seam

Clip.

Clip
after
stitching.

Clip.

Armhole seam

Side seam

Side seam

Fold under.

Cookie Cutter Doll
Instructions are on page 89.

Cookie Cutter Silver Angel
Instructions are on page 123.

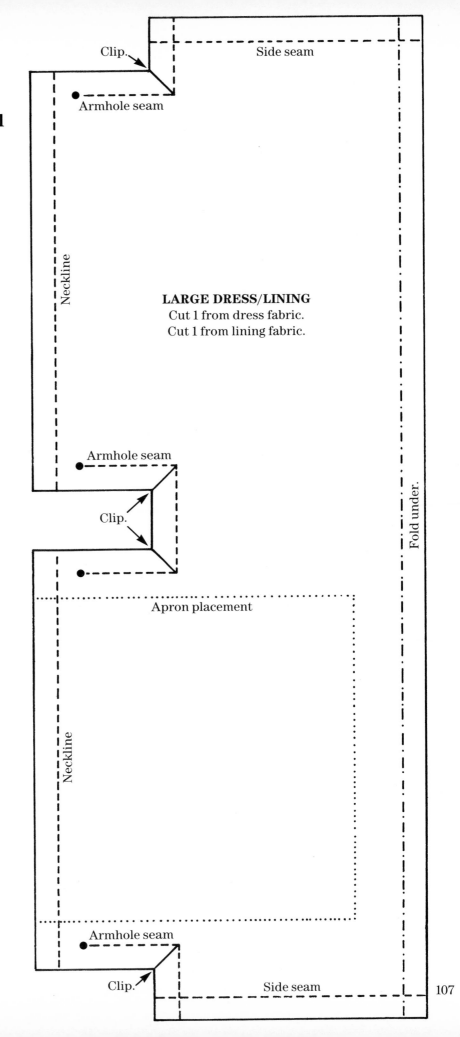

Clip.

Side seam

Armhole seam

Neckline

LARGE DRESS/LINING
Cut 1 from dress fabric.
Cut 1 from lining fabric.

Fold under.

Armhole seam

Clip.

Apron placement

PAPER DOLL

Place on fold
of paper.

Neckline

Armhole seam

Clip.

Side seam

Button Turtle

Instructions are on page 92.

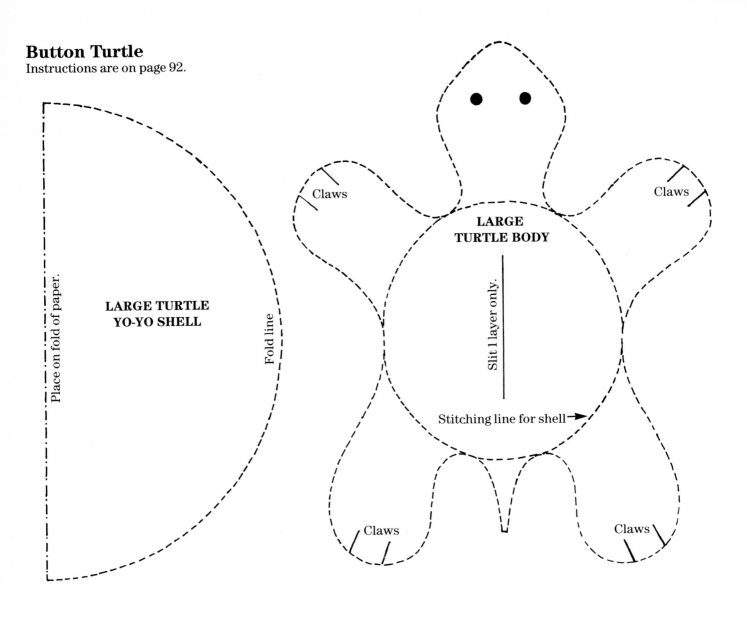

LARGE TURTLE YO-YO SHELL

Place on fold of paper.

Fold line

Claws

Claws

LARGE TURTLE BODY

Slit 1 layer only.

Stitching line for shell →

Claws

Claws

Turtle Baby

Instructions are on page 92.

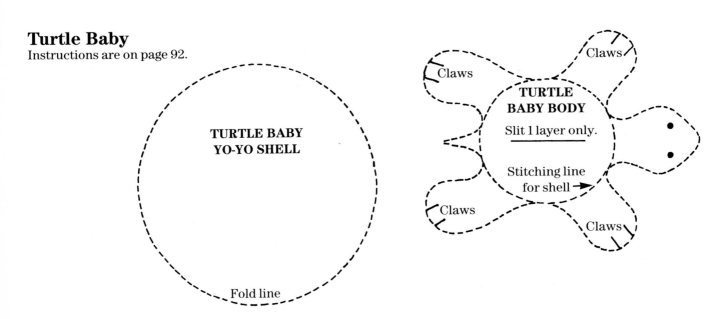

TURTLE BABY YO-YO SHELL

Fold line

Claws

Claws

TURTLE BABY BODY

Slit 1 layer only.

Stitching line for shell →

Claws

Claws

Haunted House Welcome Sign or Trick-or-Treat Bag

Instructions are on page 94.

Haunted House Pot Holder

Instructions are on page 96.

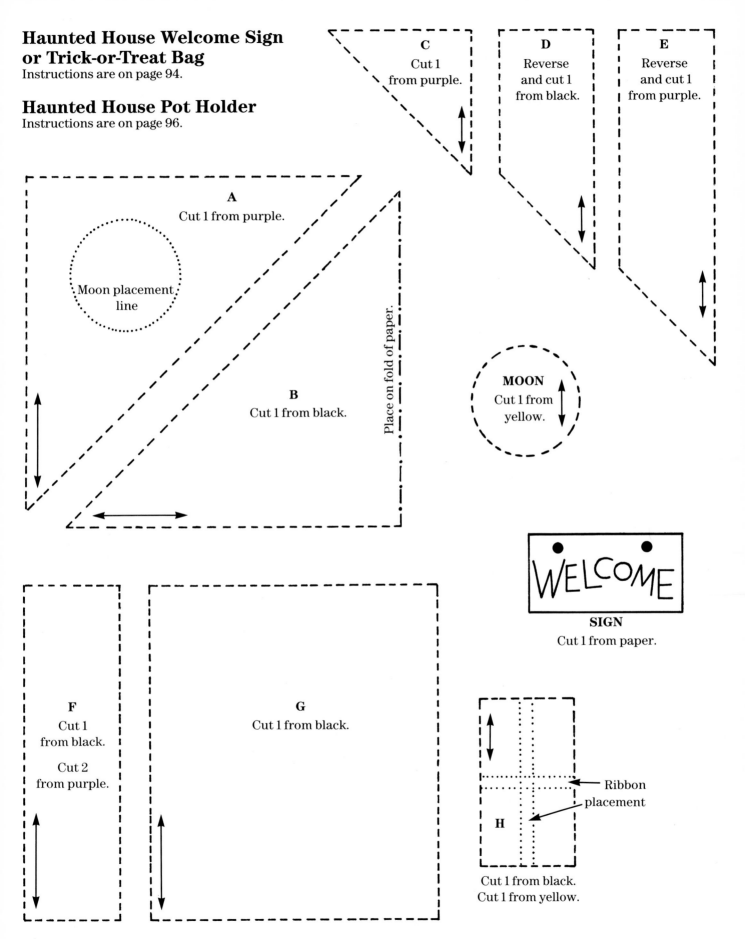

C
Cut 1
from purple.

D
Reverse
and cut 1
from black.

E
Reverse
and cut 1
from purple.

A
Cut 1 from purple.

Moon placement
line

Place on fold of paper.

B
Cut 1 from black.

MOON
Cut 1 from
yellow.

SIGN
Cut 1 from paper.

F
Cut 1
from black.

Cut 2
from purple.

G
Cut 1 from black.

H

Ribbon
placement

Cut 1 from black.
Cut 1 from yellow.

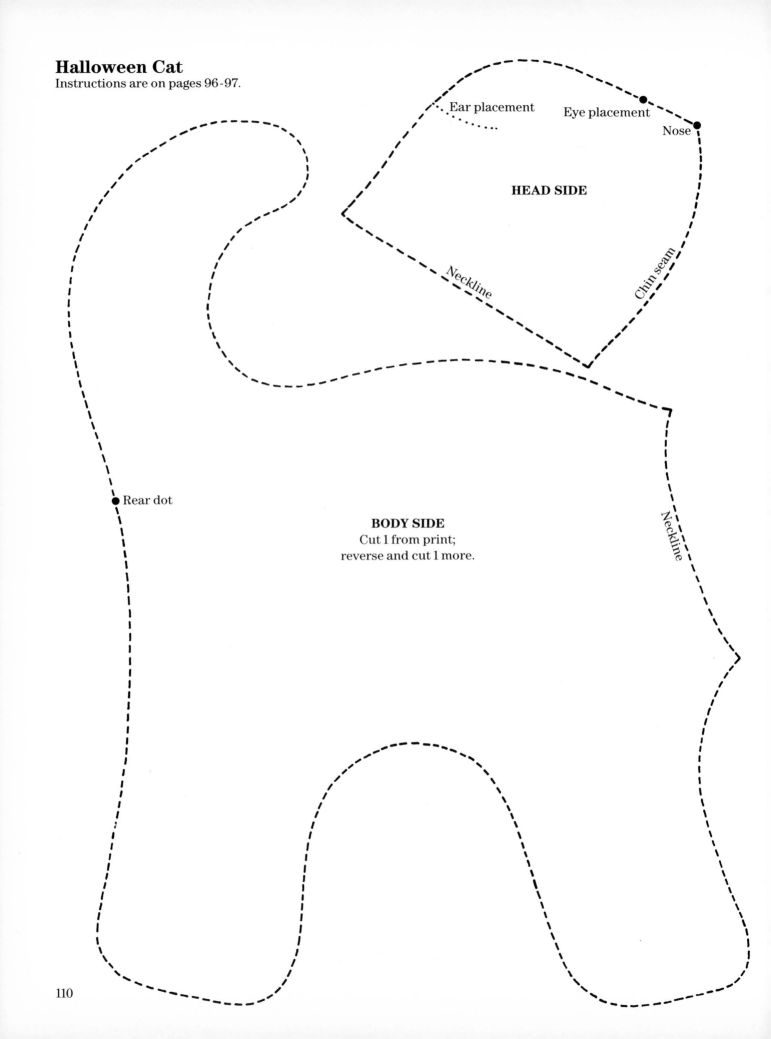

Halloween Cat
Instructions are on pages 96-97.

Ear placement

Eye placement

Nose

HEAD SIDE

Neckline

Chin seam

● Rear dot

Neckline

BODY SIDE
Cut 1 from print;
reverse and cut 1 more.

110

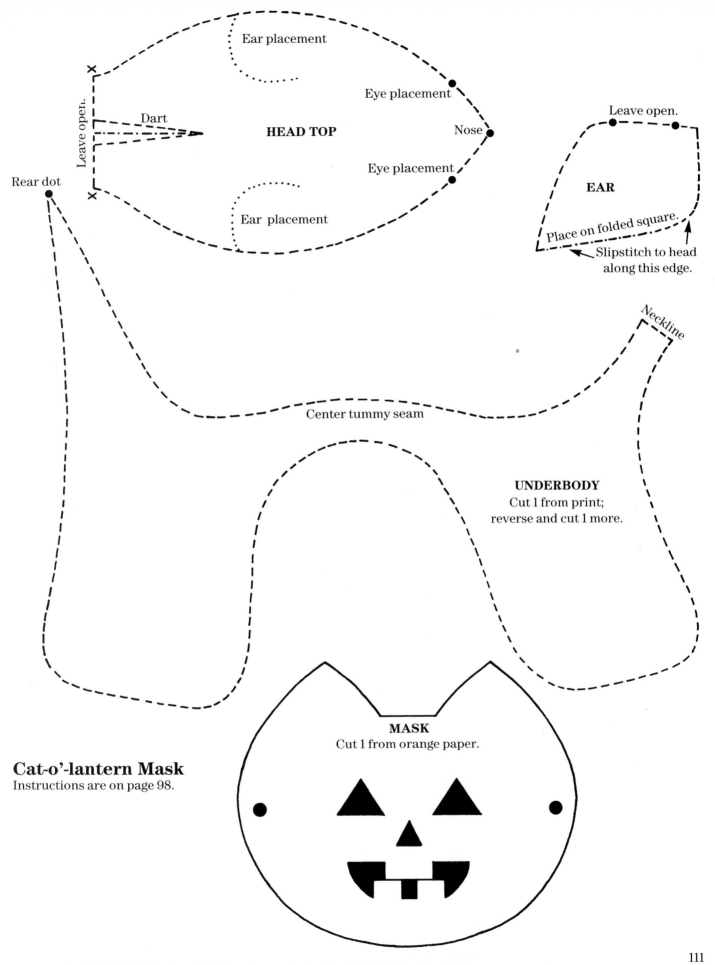

Ear placement

Eye placement

Leave open.

Dart

HEAD TOP

Nose

Eye placement

Rear dot

Ear placement

Leave open.

EAR

Place on folded square.

Slipstitch to head
along this edge.

Neckline

Center tummy seam

UNDERBODY
Cut 1 from print;
reverse and cut 1 more.

MASK
Cut 1 from orange paper.

Cat-o'-lantern Mask
Instructions are on page 98.

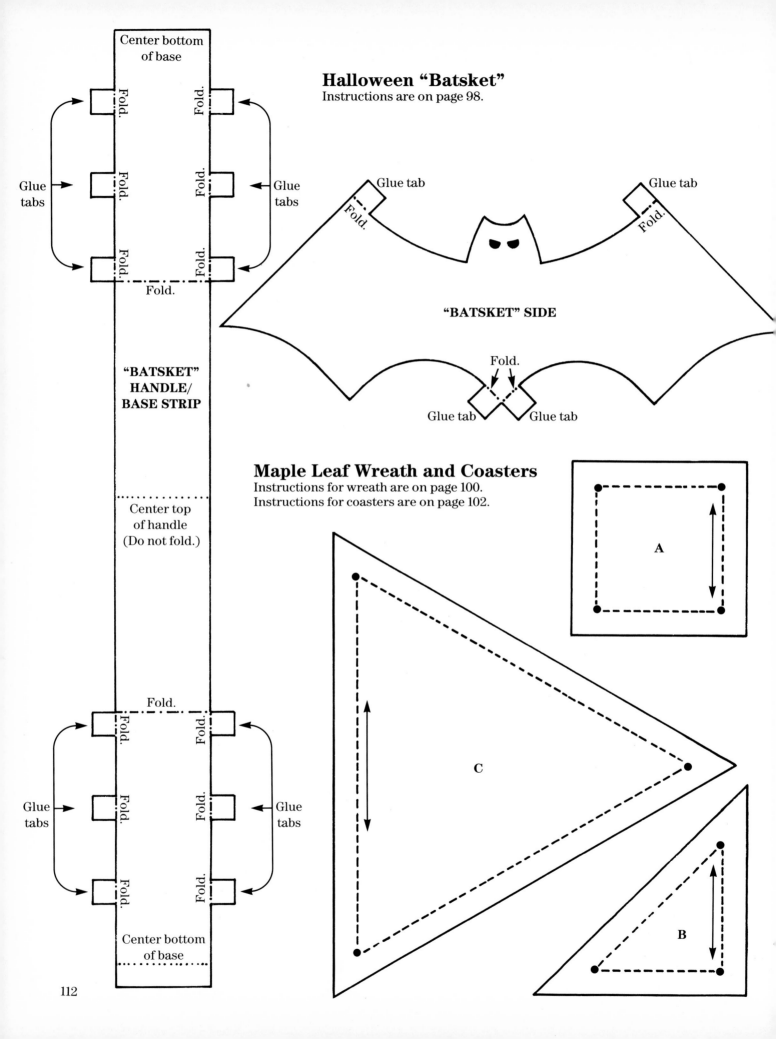

Center bottom
of base

Fold. Fold.

Glue
tabs

Fold. Fold.

Glue
tabs

Fold. Fold.

Fold.

**"BATSKET"
HANDLE/
BASE STRIP**

Center top
of handle
(Do not fold.)

Fold.

Fold. Fold.

Glue
tabs

Fold. Fold.

Glue
tabs

Fold. Fold.

Center bottom
of base

112

Halloween "Batsket"
Instructions are on page 98.

Glue tab

Fold.

Glue tab

Fold.

"BATSKET" SIDE

Fold.

Glue tab   Glue tab

Maple Leaf Wreath and Coasters
Instructions for wreath are on page 100.
Instructions for coasters are on page 102.

A

C

B

Pumpkin Nut Cup

Instructions are on page 103.

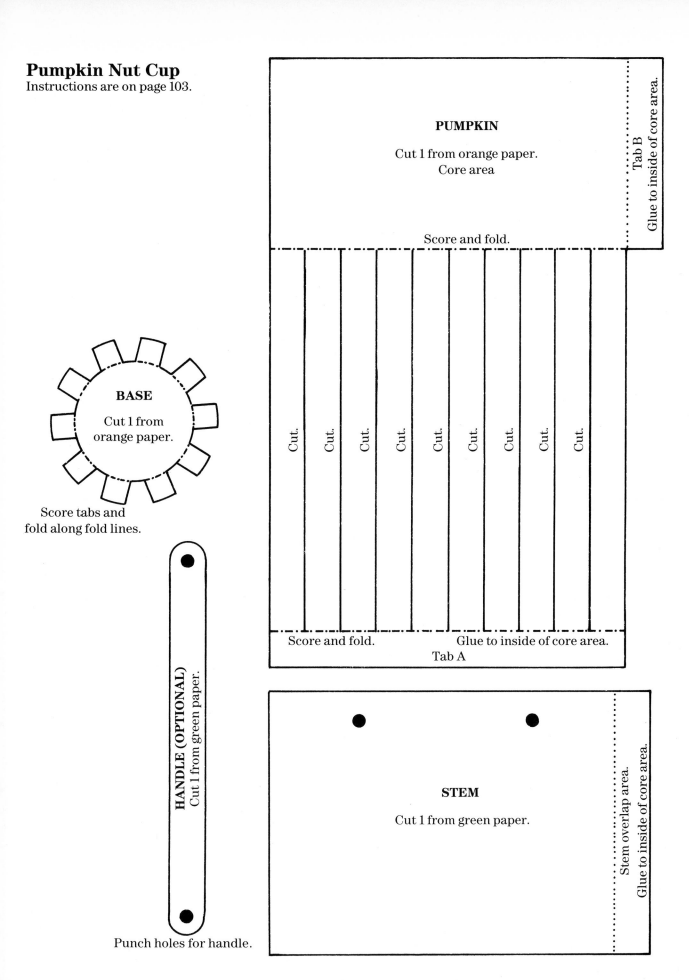

PUMPKIN

Cut 1 from orange paper.
Core area

Tab B
Glue to inside of core area.

Score and fold.

Cut. Cut. Cut. Cut. Cut. Cut. Cut. Cut. Cut.

Score and fold.   Glue to inside of core area.
Tab A

BASE

Cut 1 from
orange paper.

Score tabs and
fold along fold lines.

HANDLE (OPTIONAL)
Cut 1 from green paper.

Punch holes for handle.

STEM

Cut 1 from green paper.

Stem overlap area.
Glue to inside of core area.

HOLLY DAYS

Light candles in the darkness, hang a wreath
on the door, find the cookie cutters...winter's Holly Days
are here! Like the fresh scent of balsam, many of these projects
will bring back warm memories of happy yesterdays—letters to
Santa, clothespin figures in a crèche, snowmen, teddies,
and stockings to fill. With all of these ideas, you can
be busy creating Christmas all through the year!

From: ME

To: SANTA

WARM FRIENDS

◆

During the chilly days of winter, it's hard for children to keep up with pairs of gloves. *Another lost glove?* Don't despair, just stitch a bear! A leftover stretch-knit glove makes a simple teddy bear or baby doll. You can also use a traditional knit glove with a missing mate to fashion a handsome sweater for the bear.

Since the size and degree of stretch will vary from glove to glove, the measurements are given only as guidelines. Your eye is the best judge for the proportions, so allow each bear or baby to take on its own unique size, shape, and personality.

And if you love to crochet, you can make an easy afghan to accompany these little friends. Use your prettiest scraps of yarn or pearl cotton to fashion the doll-size granny squares.

LOST GLOVE BEAR

Materials for one bear
Pattern on page 138
1 child's or woman's stretch-knit glove (approximately 4" x 6")
2½" x 4" scrap of felt to match glove
15" (⅛"-wide) of coordinating satin ribbon (optional)
Thread to match glove
Embroidery floss: black, color to match felt
Polyester stuffing
Fabric glue

Instructions
1. Trace patterns for felt pieces, transferring markings. Cut out.

2. From felt, cut 1 muzzle, 2 paw pads, and 2 foot pads. Transfer nose on muzzle. Set pieces aside.

3. Turn glove inside out and flatten on work surface. Cut straight across to remove cuff and discard. Without stretching cut opening of glove, make small running stitches along cut edge to prevent raveling.

Referring to Diagram and handling carefully to avoid stretching, make machine-zigzag stitches from pinky crevice to top cut edge, from thumb crevice to top cut edge, and across base of middle finger. Trim glove as indicated in Diagram and set aside pieces for ears and arms.

4. Turn unit right side out. Stuff each leg firmly to measure approximately 3" long and 3" in circumference. Continue stuffing unit until measurement from bottom of legs to top cut edge is approximately 7¼". (Circumference of body should measure approximately 7".)

Diagram: Cutting and Stitching Guide

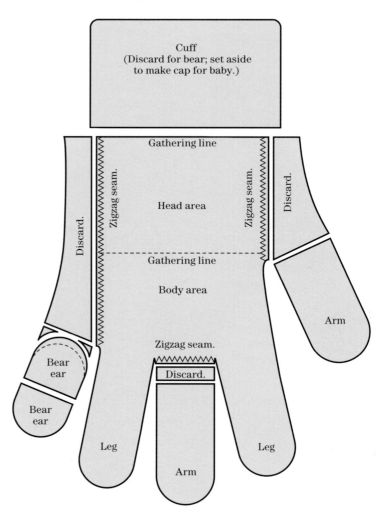

Children will love to watch as a stretch-knit glove is clipped and stitched into a Lost Glove Bear (right) or Baby (left).

Run gathering stitches around top cut edge; pull to gather, using needle to tuck raw edge inside as top is gathered. Tie off securely. Tightly slip-stitch sides of gathered area together to close neatly.

5. To define head, use doubled thread to run gathering stitches around center of body as indicated in Diagram. Pull thread tightly to gather. Knot securely; then wrap thread around gathered neck several times and knot securely.

To define legs, wrap doubled thread tightly at an angle around top of each leg and knot securely.

6. To make arms, use reserved glove middle finger and thumb. Trim both to same length; if thumb is wider than finger, run zigzag stitches along length to decrease width. Turn both right side out. Stuff and stretch each to measure approximately 2½" long and about 2½" in circumference. Run gathering stitches around opening on 1 piece, close to cut edge.

Pull to gather, using needle to tuck cut edge inside as arm is gathered. Tie off securely and slipstitch sides of gathered area together to close neatly. Repeat with remaining arm.

Place 1 arm on each side of body, ¼" from neck; slipstitch each securely to body.

Referring to photo, lightly glue paw pads in place. Using 2 strands of matching floss, secure pads in place

Continued on page 118

Continued from page 117

with small blanket stitches. To define wrists, wrap doubled thread tightly around each arm just above pad and knot securely.

7. To make feet, on each leg, place pin horizontally ⁷⁄₈" from bottom; fold at pin and slipstitch foot securely in folded position. Add foot pads in same manner as paw pads. To define ankles, wrap doubled thread tightly around legs at fold and knot securely.

8. To make ears, use reserved tip and cut piece from pinky. Turn unstitched cut piece to wrong side; make running stitches along rounded end and trim (see Diagram). Turn both ears to right side and run gathering stitches along each open edge. For each, pull to gather tightly and overcast edges together securely. Flatten each ear and, referring to photo, slipstitch each ear in place.

9. To make muzzle, fold felt piece, aligning straight edges. Machine-stitch close to straight edges, forming a cone. Turn right side out and stuff lightly. With seam at bottom, center muzzle on head, ⅛" above neck, and pin in place. Using 2 strands of matching floss, secure muzzle to head with small blanket stitches. Using 1 strand of black floss, satin-stitch triangle for nose and ⅛"-diameter circles for eyes; then make 1 straight stitch on seam for nose line and 2 straight stitches angled down for mouth.

If desired, tie ribbon in bow around bear's neck.

SWEATER BEAR

Materials for one bear
Pattern on page 138
All materials listed for Lost Glove Bear
1 child's or woman's traditional knit patterned glove (approximately 3" x 8")
Thread to match patterned glove

Instructions

1. Refer to Steps 1–5 of Lost Glove Bear, pages 116–117. Set aside.

2. Turn patterned glove wrong side out. Stitch across base of thumb. Cut off thumb and discard.

Turn glove to right side. If desired, cut off cuff portion and set aside for turtleneck. (Alternately, cuff can be left on to form finished bottom edge of sweater.) Cut straight across to remove fingers and set aside for sleeves and cuffs. Handling carefully to avoid stretching, make small running stitches along all cut edges to prevent raveling.

3. Carefully slip trimmed glove over bear body. Along top cut edge, turn under ¼" and run gathering stitches. Pull to gather snugly around neckline and knot securely. On bottom edge, turn hem under to desired length and stitch securely; or, if cuff has been left on, roll up cuff and tack to sweater.

To make optional turtleneck, turn cuff ring to wrong side; make small running stitches along cut edge. Tie off. Carefully pull over bear's head and whipstitch cut edge to sweater at neckline. Fold finished edge down.

4. To make arms, follow Step 6 of Lost Glove Bear, but *do not stitch arms to body.* Cut off tips from 2 reserved glove fingers and discard. Make small running stitches along cut edges, and pull 1 over each finished arm.

Run gathering stitches around each wrist and pull to gather. Turn each remaining cut edge under and slipstitch to end of each arm.

To make cuffs, cut 2 glove fingers to make 2 (1½"-long) cylinders. For each cuff, turn each cut edge under to make ½"-wide cuff ring. Securely slipstitch 1 to each sleeve. Slipstitch each arm to body.

LOST GLOVE BABY

Materials for one baby
Pattern on page 138
1 child's or woman's stretch-knit glove (approximately 4" x 6")
3½" square of tan, pink, or brown felt for face
11" (⅜"-wide) of coordinating grosgrain ribbon for scarf
Thread to match
Embroidery floss for eyes, mouth, and hair
Polyester stuffing
1 (1") and 2 (½") white or colored acrylic pom-poms (optional)
Powder blush
Cotton swab

Instructions

1. Trace pattern for face, transferring markings. Cut out.

2. On felt, trace 1 face, transferring facial features. Using 2 strands of floss in desired colors, satin-stitch eyes and backstitch mouth. Cut out face and set aside.

3. Refer to Steps 3–7 of Lost Glove Bear, beginning on page 116, to make baby, reserving trimmed cuff, discarding pinky, and omitting paw pads and foot pads.

4. To add face, align bottom edge of felt with gathered neckline. With thread to match face, attach face to neckline with small overcast stitches at ⅛" intervals.

5. To make cap, clip stitches along base of folded cuff and open cuff along fold. Turn opened cuff inside out; make small running stitches along 1 cut edge to prevent raveling. Run gathering stitches along remaining open edge, pull tightly to gather, and knot securely. Turn cap to right side and slipstitch sides of gathered area together to secure. Place cap on head; turn under cut edge, overlapping face. With thread to match cap, slipstitch folded edge of cap to face.

To add hair, using floss in desired color, make looped stitches just under edge of cap around top of face. Leave loops for curls or clip threads to make straight hair.

If desired, tack large pom-pom to top of hat at gathered area; tack small pom-poms to top of each foot. *Do not add pom-poms if toy is for child under 3 years old.*

CROCHETED MINIATURE AFGHAN

Materials
78 yards of assorted colors of crewel
  yarn *or* 87 yards of assorted colors
  of size 3 pearl cotton for squares
80 yards of black crewel yarn *or* 98
  yards of white size 3 pearl cotton
  for joining and edging
Size 3 steel crochet hook for yarn
  afghan *or* size 2 steel crochet hook
  for pearl cotton afghan
Note: Refer to photo on page 160 for
  pearl cotton afghan.

Crochet Abbreviations
beg—beginning
ch—chain
dc—double crochet
lp—loop
rep—repeat
rnd(s)—round(s)
sc—single crochet
sl st—slip stitch
sp—space

Instructions
Note: Use thread colors as desired to crochet rnds 1 and 2 of each square. Make 25 squares for 1 afghan. Use 1 strand of crewel yarn for crocheting.

First square: With first color, ch 6, join with a sl st to form a ring. **Rnd 1:** Ch 3 for first dc, 2 dc in ring, (ch 2, 3 dc in ring) 3 times, ch 2, sl st in top of beg ch-3. Fasten off. **Rnd 2:** Join 2nd color with sl st in any ch-2 sp, ch 3 for first dc, (2 dc, ch 2, 3 dc) in same sp, * ch 2, (3 dc, ch 2, 3 dc) in next ch-2 sp, rep from * twice more, ch 2, sl st in top of beg ch-3. Fasten off. **Rnd 3:** Join joining color with sl st in any corner sp, ch 3 for first dc, (2 dc, ch 2, 3 dc) in same corner sp, * ch 2, 3 dc in next ch-2 sp, ch 2, (3 dc, ch 2, 3 dc) in next corner sp, rep from * twice more, ch 2, 3 dc in next ch-2 sp, ch 2, sl st in top of beg ch-3. Fasten off.

2nd square: With first color, ch 6, join with a sl st to form a ring. **Rnds 1 and 2:** Rep rnds 1 and 2 as for first square. **Rnd 3** (joining rnd): Join joining color with sl st in any corner sp, ch 3 for first dc, (2 dc, ch 2, 3 dc) in same corner sp, ch 2, 3 dc in next ch-2 sp, ch 2, (3 dc, ch 2, 3 dc) in next corner sp, ch 2, 3 dc in next ch-2 sp,

ch 2, 3 dc in next corner sp, ch 1 drop lp from hook, insert hook in corner sp on first square, pick up dropped lp and pull through, ch 1, 3 dc in same corner sp on 2nd square, ch 1, join in next ch-2 sp on first square as before, ch 1, 3 dc in next ch-2 sp on 2nd square, ch 1, join in next ch-2 sp on first square as before, ch 1, 3 dc in next corner sp on 2nd square, ch 1, join in next corner sp on first square as before, ch 1, 3 dc in same corner sp on 2nd square, ch 2, 3 dc in next ch-2 sp on 2nd square, ch 2, sl st in top of beg ch-3. Fasten off.

Continue to make and join squares in same manner for an afghan 5 squares wide and 5 squares long.

Edging: Join edging color with sl st in any corner of afghan, sc in same sp, ch 2, sl st in top of sc just made for picot, sc in same corner sp, * (sc in each of next 3 dc, ch 2, sl st in top of sc just made for picot, sc in next ch-2 sp) twice, sc in each of next 3 dc, ch 2, sl st in top of sc just made for

picot, rep from * across to 3 dc before next corner sp, sc in each of 3 dc, sc in corner, ch 2, sl st in top of sc just made for picot, sc in same corner, rep from * around, end with sl st in beg sc. Fasten off. Weave in all thread ends.

FAMILY FAVORITES

◆

A piece of stretch-knit terry cloth cut from a mateless sock could be the beginning of a cheerful "Snowfamily." Make the Snowmom along with her own Snowbaby snuggled in her arms. Create a Snowdad and baby in the same manner, by using black grosgrain ribbon for the hats and omitting the satin ribbon rose. And for a special holiday accessory to wear, just add a pin to the back of a Snowbaby.

Winter evenings by the fire are a wonderful time to stitch old-time yo-yos to make a jolly Santa, complete with his bag of fragrant balsam fir tips. You can turn a cookie cutter into a shimmering silver angel. Or let your family help to create a simple crèche with its figures made from clothespins.

SNOWMOM AND SNOWBABY

Materials
Pattern on page 138
4½" x 10" piece of white stretch sport sock with terry cloth lining
6¼" (1½"-wide) of red grosgrain ribbon for large hat crown
16" (⅝"-wide) of red grosgrain ribbon for large hat brim and small hat crown
6½" (⅜"-wide) of red grosgrain ribbon for small hat brim
10" (⅜"-wide) of red-and-green stripe grosgrain ribbon for large scarf
5" (⅛"-wide) of red-and-green stripe grosgrain ribbon for small scarf
Thread to match
Black embroidery floss
Vanishing fabric marker
Polyester stuffing
White satin ribbon rose with leaves

Instructions for one Snowmom
Note: For Snowmom and Snowbaby, terry cloth side of stretch knit will always be considered to be *right* side. All seams should be ⅛", and all gathering stitches should be made using doubled thread.

1. Trace pattern pieces, transferring markings. Cut out.

2. From stretch-knit terry cloth, cut 1 body piece and 1 arm piece, transferring markings. Set aside scraps.

3. With right sides facing, fold body piece on marked fold line. Stitch together along center back raw edge. Run gathering stitches around 1 short edge of body piece. Pull thread to gather tightly; tie off securely and turn.

Stuff body and stretch to measure 5" long and 6½" in circumference. Run gathering stitches along raw edge. Pull to gather tightly and tie off. To shape head, run gathering stitches around body 1¾" from top; pull tightly and tie off. For neck, repeat ⅛" below gathering line for head.

To define legs, using doubled thread and stitching back and forth through all layers, make 1"-long vertical line of stitches up from center bottom edge. Set aside.

4. On each short end of arm piece, turn under ⅛" and hem. With right sides facing, fold arm piece in half on fold line. Stitch along long raw edge; turn. Referring to pattern, run gathering stitches around circumference of arm piece at center. Pull tightly to gather and tie off. Stuff and stretch each side until arm piece measures 4½" long and 2½" in circumference. Run gathering stitches along raw edge of each open end; pull each to gather tightly and tie off. Referring to photo, slipstitch each end of arm piece to body just below neckline.

5. For hat brim, cut 12½" of ⅝"-wide ribbon. Set aside remainder for Snowbaby hat crown. Run gathering stitches along length of ribbon close to 1 edge. Pull to gather to measure 6¼"; tie off.

Along 1 long edge of 1½"-wide ribbon, butt gathered edge of ⅝"-wide ribbon; whipstitch edges together.

With right sides facing, fold ribbon pieces widthwise and machine stitch short edges together. Turn right side

out. Run gathering stitches along remaining long edge of 1½"-wide ribbon; pull to gather and tie off, forming hat. With seam of hat at back, place hat on head and tack to back at neckline. Tack ribbon rose to side of hat.

6. Referring to photo and using fabric marker, draw facial features.

Using 2 strands of floss, satin-stitch eyes and make French knots for mouth. Tie ³/₈"-wide stripe ribbon around neck.

Instructions for one Snowbaby
1. Trace circle pattern and cut out.
2. From stretch-knit terry cloth scraps, cut 2 circles.

3. Run gathering stitches around 1 circle. Pull to gather partially; stuff firmly. Pull to gather tightly, forming a small sphere, and tie off. Repeat with remaining circle. With gathered areas facing, securely slipstitch spheres together.
4. Using ³/₈"-wide red ribbon for gathered hat brim and remaining

⁵/₈"-wide ribbon for hat crown, refer to Step 5 of Snowmom to make small hat, omitting ribbon rose. Referring to Step 6 and using 1 strand of floss, embroider facial features. Tie ¹/₈"-wide stripe ribbon around neck. Tuck baby in Snowmom's arms.

YO-YO SANTA

Materials

Pattern on page 139
4" square of white knit T-shirt fabric
    for head
3½" x 5½" piece of red knit T-shirt
    fabric for hat
2½" x 6½" piece of peach fabric for
    face and hands
4" x 8" piece of black fabric for belt
    and boots
6" square of red-and-white print
    fabric for collar
29 (4") squares of assorted
    red-and-white print fabrics
    for yo-yos
5½" x 7" piece of green print fabric
    for bag
Thread to match
Embroidery floss: black, light peach,
    bright peach, and red for facial
    features, 1 full skein of white for
    beard
Polyester stuffing
¾" white acrylic pom-pom
Extra-fine unwaxed dental floss
Green string for bag ties
Balsam fir tips
Note: See Resources, page 159.

Instructions

1. Trace pattern pieces, transferring markings. Cut out.

2. On right side of peach fabric, trace pattern for 1 face and 2 hands, transferring markings. *Do not cut out yet.* Set aside.

On wrong side of black fabric, trace 1 small yo-yo pattern for belt and cut out. With right sides facing, fold remaining black fabric in half; pin layers together and trace 2 boots, transferring markings. *Do not cut out yet.* Set aside.

Cut remaining pieces as indicated on pattern and transfer markings.

3. To make large yo-yo for collar, turn under ¼" around edge of large fabric circle. Thread needle with dental floss; run gathering stitches close to folded edge of circle, stitching through both layers of fabric. Pull floss tightly to gather and tie off. Flatten yo-yo, centering opening; distribute gathers evenly.

Repeat, using smaller circles, to make 1 black yo-yo for belt and 29 red-and-white yo-yos for body, arms, and legs. Set aside.

4. To make head, use dental floss to run gathering stitches ¼" around edge of white knit circle. Pull to gather partially; stuff firmly. Pull to gather tightly. (Head circumference

should measure 4¾".) Tie floss to secure. Roll head in palms to shape. Set aside.

5. On right side of traced face on peach fabric, stitch facial features. Using 1 strand of embroidery floss, make black satin stitches for eyes, light peach satin stitches for nose, and bright peach satin stitches for cheeks. Using 1 strand of red floss, backstitch mouth.

Cut out face and 2 hands. Referring to Step 4 above, make 2 small spheres for hands, each measuring 1¾" in circumference. For each hand, pinch gathered seam allowance and tack together, forming a stem. Set aside.

With gathered area of head at center back, center face on front of head sphere. Overcast raw edges of face to head. Set aside.

6. To make braided beard, remove label from skein of white floss. Open skein and carefully separate floss to make a ring. Tie 6" length of thread around floss at top. Clip floss at bottom of ring.

Tape ends of thread at top of ring to work surface. Divide strands of floss into 3 sections and make ½"-wide flat braid. Slipstitch beard to face from dot to dot along marked placement line.

7. To make hat, with right sides facing and raw edges aligned, fold red knit fabric in half widthwise to measure 3½" x 2¾"; stitch along long edge. Run gathering stitches along 1 open edge; pull to gather tightly and tie off securely; turn. Tack pom-pom to gathered area.

Fold remaining raw edge ⅜" to right side of hat and baste loosely. Fold again to form cuff. Place small amount of stuffing inside top of hat. With seam at back, place hat on head. Align edge of hat cuff just under edge of beard, covering raw edge of peach fabric. Pull front of hat down to cover each end of beard. Tack hat to head at center bottom just under beard. Unfold cuff and slipstitch hat to face. Refold cuff. Set aside.

8. To make boots, machine-stitch each boot along traced seam line, leaving open where indicated on pattern. Cut out each boot. For each, trim stitched seam allowance to ⅛". Clip curves and turn. Stuff firmly.

Run gathering stitches along raw edge; pull tightly to gather and tie off. Pinch seam allowance at top of boot and tack together, forming a stem.

9. Insert stem of 1 boot into center opening of 1 small red-and-white yo-yo. Slipstitch gathered edge of yo-yo to gathered edge of boot. Repeat with remaining boot.

To make 1 leg, thread needle with dental floss. Insert needle through boot top and open center of small red-and-white yo-yo, concealing knot inside yo-yo opening and exiting at center back. Add 6 more yo-yos, stitching through each open center to center back.

Compress stack gently to measure 1¾", tie off securely at center of top yo-yo. Remove needle, leaving long floss tail. Repeat to make remaining leg.

In same manner, make 2 stacks for arms, beginning each with a peach fabric hand and stacking 6 yo-yos to measure 1½".

10. To make body, insert needle through open center of large collar yo-yo, concealing knot inside yo-yo opening and exiting at center back. Stitching through each open center to center back, add 2 small red-and-white yo-yos, black yo-yo, and remaining red-and-white yo-yo, stacking to measure 1¼". Tie off.

11. To assemble Santa, place head on collar yo-yo, aligning yo-yo opening with hat center back seam, just behind cuff of hat. Slipstitch in place. Securely tie tails of arms together under collar, leaving about 1" between arms. Tie tails to dental floss joining body yo-yos and trim tails of arms. Securely tie tails of legs together and to bottom of dental floss joining body. Set aside.

12. To make bag, cut green fabric in half widthwise to measure 5½" x 3½". With right sides facing and raw edges aligned, machine-stitch around 3 edges, leaving 1 short edge open. Clip corners and turn. Turn under 1½" along top edge. Mark stitching line 1" and 1¼" from fold. Using string, run gathering stitches along each marked line. Fill bag with balsam. Pull strings tightly to gather bag and tie. Knot ends of strings together and wrap ties around Santa's hand.

COOKIE CUTTER SILVER ANGEL

Materials
Pattern on page 107
2 (5" x 11") pieces of silver fabric for dress and lining
11" (4"-wide) of white lace for overskirt
4½" (⅜"-wide) of looped silver trim for halo
24" (¼"-wide) of silver ribbon
Thread to match
5"-tall girl or boy cookie cutter, approximately 3¼" wide and 1" deep*
Vanishing fabric marker
Tiny safety pin
Craft glue
5"-diameter silver paper doily
12" of silver thread and 10 (¾"-wide) silver stars for garland (optional)
*Note: See Resources, page 159.

Instructions
1. Centering looped trim on sharp edge of cookie cutter, glue to head for halo.

2. Trace pattern, adding ¼" along bottom edge of dress/lining piece, and transferring markings. Cut out.

Cut 1 dress piece and 1 lining piece. With right sides up and raw edges aligned, baste lace for overskirt to dress piece along neckline edges. (Lace will extend across armholes.)

3. To assemble dress, refer to Steps 4–5 of Cookie Cutter Doll, page 89, omitting apron. After stitching armhole seams, trim excess lace. (To avoid raveling silver fabric, do not trim seams; do clip into corners.)

To finish dress, refer to Steps 6–8 of Cookie Cutter Doll, omitting lace along hem, omitting bonnet, and leaving seams untrimmed.

4. To make wings, with wrong sides facing, fold doily in half. Aligning folded edge of doily with top edge of dress, glue doily to center back.

To make optional garland, center thread on wrong side of 5 stars; match and glue remaining stars on top to secure thread. Insert ends of thread into "hands" of cookie cutter and glue each end to back of cutter.

CLOTHESPIN CRECHE

Materials

Pattern on page 140
1 (3½" x 5½") piece each of 2
    different print fabrics
1" square of brown felt
5" x 8" piece of white felt
2 (3⅜" x 5⅜") pieces of medium-
    weight fusible interfacing
1 skein of green embroidery floss
14" square of corrugated cardboard
4" square of tan art paper
Craft knife
White glue
2" square of gold foil paper *or* 2" gold
    foil star
1 round toothpick
Transparent tape
3 round-top wooden clothespins
Small handsaw
File or rasp
Fine-point marker: black, red
Vanishing fabric marker
3 (1¼") gold notary seals
Pinking shears (optional)
Fine straw

Instructions

1. Trace pattern pieces, transferring markings. Cut out.

2. Referring to Diagram for measurements, lightly mark corrugated cardboard for stable, roof, and floor pieces. Cut out. If desired, gently peel away 1 layer of paper on roof to expose corrugations.

Score and fold each stable side where indicated on pattern. Insert floor and glue in place. Aligning back edges of roof with stable and extending roof ⅛" beyond stable on each side, glue roof in place.

Cut star from gold foil using pattern or use purchased gold star. Tape toothpick to back of star; then tape other end of toothpick to back of stable at center top.

3. To make manger, from tan art paper, cut 1 manger and 2 manger legs. Referring to pattern, cut slits in manger. Score and fold manger along center line, forming a V. Insert 1 leg into each slit at each end of manger.

4. To make figures, use saw to trim 2 clothespins to each measure 3¼" long for Mary and Joseph and 1 clothespin to measure 1¼" long for baby. Referring to photo, use black marker to make 2 dots for eyes and red marker to make thin, curved line for mouth on all faces. Set aside.

5. For Mary, following manufacturer's instructions, center interfacing on wrong side of 1 print fabric and fuse together. Mark robe pattern on interfacing and cut out.

Apply glue to glue tab and around neckline. Wrap robe around 1 clothespin, pressing neckline to ease fullness and holding center back of robe until dry. From white felt, cut full-length mantle. Run line of glue down center back, butt edges together, and hold until dry. Apply glue to top of clothespin head. Place mantle on head and press to shape. Let dry. Center and glue right side of notary seal to back of head for halo.

From floss, cut 3 (11") pieces. Tie pieces together 1" from 1 end. Tape tied end to work surface. Braid 7" length and knot floss ends together 1" from remaining end, leaving fringe. Tie around figure, with knot centered at front. Trim fringe to ½".

6. For Joseph, refer to Step 5, using remaining print fabric and cutting short mantle from white felt. Cut beard from brown felt and glue in place.

7. For baby, cut blanket from remaining white felt, using pinking shears if desired. Place clothespin baby diagonally on blanket. Fold bottom corner up to chin. Overlap side corners at front, easing in fullness.

Cut 10" length of floss. Referring to photo, wrap floss around baby at foot area, crossing in back and again in front, and tying at back of neck. Trim floss tails. Center and glue right side of notary seal to back of head for halo.

8. Fill manger with straw; sprinkle straw on floor and around stable. Place baby in manger and arrange remaining figures as desired.

Diagram: Cutting Crèche

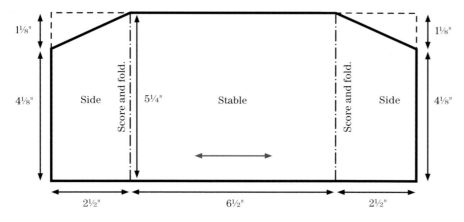

Red arrows show direction of cardboard corrugations.

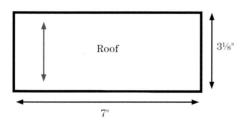

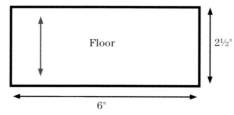

Y*ear after year, your family will look forward to displaying this simple crèche made from corrugated cardboard, clothespins, and scraps of fabric.*

125

SANTA CLOTHES ORNAMENTS

◆

What fun it is to stitch tiny boots and hang Santa's clothes on miniature hangers! Use good quality felt, pretty decorative ribbon, and your neatest blanket stitches to craft these special decorations.

SANTA'S TROUSERS ORNAMENT

Materials
Pattern on page 141
5" x 9¾" piece of red felt
5" x 10¾" piece of white felt
23" (⅜"-wide) of decorative ribbon
Thread to match
White embroidery floss
4 (¼") bells or buttons
12" green chenille stem

Instructions
Note: Pattern includes ⅛" seam allowances.

1. Trace pattern pieces, transferring markings. Cut out.

2. Fold red felt in half lengthwise to measure 2½" x 9¾". Place trousers pattern on fold and trace 2, transferring markings. Cut out. Unfold each piece and stack, aligning raw edges. Stitch each curved center seam (see Diagram 1). Clip curves. Referring to Diagram 2, rotate seams and align at front and back. To make trousers legs, stitch inseam. Turn right side out. Around waist, turn under ¼" and baste. Set aside.

3. Fold white felt in half lengthwise to measure 2½" x 10¾". Place trousers lining pattern on fold and trace 2, transferring markings. Cut out. Mark cuff fold line with basting stitches. Clip seam allowances to X where indicated on pattern. Stitch in same manner as trousers. Do not turn.

4. With wrong sides facing, insert lining into trousers, aligning front and back seams and folded waistband edges. At bottom of each leg, fold and pin excess lining to right side of trousers along basted placement lines. Using 2 strands of floss, secure lining to each leg with small blanket stitches.

5. Cut ribbon in half. With wrong sides facing, stitch ribbons together along each long edge. Cut stitched ribbon in half. Referring to marked placement dots at front of trousers, insert 1 end of each ribbon ½" into waistband, between layers, and tack in place.

Crossing ribbons, insert remaining ends into waistband at back, aligning each with marked placement dots; tack. Stitching through 1 layer only, attach bells or buttons to front and back of trousers just below ribbons at waistband. Slipstitch waistband layers together.

6. To make hanger, tightly fold back ¼" of chenille stem to eliminate sharp end. Beginning with folded end, place stem directly on Diagram 3 and bend to match shape. Wrap remaining end of stem around hook several times to secure. Place trousers on hanger.

Diagram 1: Stitching Center Seams

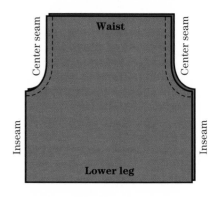

Diagram 2: Aligning Center Seams and Stitching Inseams

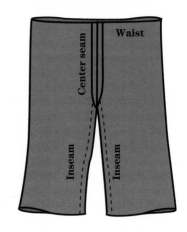

Diagram 3: Shaping Hanger

Folded end of chenille stem →

← Wrap remaining end of chenille stem around hooked end.

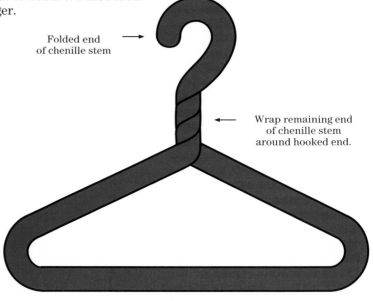

SANTA'S JACKET ORNAMENT

Materials

Pattern on pages 141–142
8½" square of red felt
9" x 11" piece of white felt
Thread to match
White embroidery floss
8 (¼") bells or buttons
12" green chenille stem

Instructions

Note: Pattern includes ⅛" seam allowances.

1. On folded paper, trace pattern pieces, transferring markings. Cut out.

2. From red felt, cut 1 jacket, transferring markings with basting stitches. From white felt, cut 1 lining and 1 collar, clipping each side of collar where indicated on pattern.

3. Aligning raw edges, fold jacket at shoulders. Machine-stitch each side/underarm seam. Clip almost to seam along each side/underarm. Turn and finger-press. Repeat to make lining, but do not turn.

4. With wrong sides facing, carefully insert lining into jacket, avoiding stretching. Align raw edges of jacket and lining at neckline and baste together ⅜" from raw edges.

5. Beginning along lower edge of jacket, fold excess lining to right side of jacket, aligning with basted placement line. Baste in place. Using 2 strands of floss, secure lining to jacket with small blanket stitches. Repeat with each sleeve; then repeat with center front edges.

6. Around basted neck edge, clip almost to basting at ¼" intervals. On collar, turn short edges under ¼" and baste. Aligning 1 long edge of collar with marked placement line on right side of jacket, baste together; then secure with small blanket stitches. Repeat to join remaining long edge of collar to lining, adjusting turned-under short edges to align with jacket front edges, if necessary. Slipstitch openings closed.

7. Referring to photo, evenly space and sew 4 buttons or bells on each side of jacket front.

To make hanger, refer to Step 6 of Santa's Trousers Ornament. Place jacket on hanger.

SANTA'S BOOTS ORNAMENT

Materials for one pair

Pattern on page 141
8" square of green felt
8" (⅜"-wide) of decorative ribbon
Thread to match
Green embroidery floss
Polyester stuffing
White pencil
8" of red string or pearl cotton

Instructions

Note: Pattern includes ⅛" seam allowances.

1. Trace pattern pieces, transferring markings. Cut out.

2. From felt, cut 2 each of boot upper, boot sole, and boot vamp. Transfer markings. Set aside scraps.

3. Cut ribbon in half. Referring to marked placement lines, align 1 piece along each boot upper. Machine-stitch along each long edge.

4. Referring to pattern, clip lower edge of 1 boot upper. Overlap boot upper with vamp, matching small center dots; baste, stitching from each side toward center. Using 2 strands of floss, make small blanket stitches to secure vamp to boot upper. Repeat with remaining boot upper and vamp.

5. With right sides facing and long raw edges aligned, fold each boot unit in half. Machine-stitch each along long edge. Carefully turn.

Fold each boot along top edge of ribbon, tucking lining area inside boot.

6. Align sole along bottom of each boot, matching large dots at center front and X with center back seam; baste. Make small blanket stitches to secure edges together. Lightly stuff foot of each boot. Insert small scrap of felt inside boot to cover stuffing.

Stitch 1 end of string or pearl cotton to center back of each boot at top edge.

WOOLLY NEIGHBORS

◆

This wreath with its friendly menagerie derives a special charm from the rich, warm tones of the wool. Disregarding every "wool rule," fabric pieces are machine-washed in warm water and laundry detergent and then tossed in the dryer! The result is soft, fuzzy, dense wool with an antique patina.

FRIENDLY NEIGHBORS WREATH

Materials
Pattern on pages 143–145
Note: The fabric should be measured only after washing and drying.
18" x 37" piece of black washed wool
16" x 24" piece of maroon washed wool
7" x 11" piece of antique gold washed wool
5" x 11" piece of green washed wool
6" (⅛"-wide) of black grosgrain ribbon
22" (¼"-wide) of black double-fold bias tape
Thread to match
4 skeins of golden brown pearl cotton
Polyester stuffing
Sharp embroidery scissors
White pencil
Large embroidery needle

Instructions
1. On folded paper, trace wreath top pattern and wreath bottom pattern, transferring markings. Cut out each. Matching dots, tape wreath top and wreath bottom patterns together. Trace remaining pieces, transferring markings. Cut out.

2. From black wool, cut 1 (18") square. Centering wreath pattern on right side of wool, use white pencil to transfer pattern and markings. Staystitch along seam lines around outside and inside of wreath. Cut outer edge of wreath, but *do not cut out center yet.* Set aside.

3. Cut maroon wool in half lengthwise to yield 2 (8" x 24") pieces. On right side of 1 piece, trace 24 closely placed scallops, transferring markings. With wrong sides facing, layer marked piece on remaining piece of maroon wool. Using 2 pins inside each traced scallop, pin layers together. Cut out each pair of scallops, leaving pins in place; set aside scraps.

Using pearl cotton, make blanket stitches around curved edge of each pair of scallops, leaving edge marked for seam line open. Staystitch along each marked seam line. Clip seam allowances at ⅛" intervals. Set aside.

4. From maroon wool scraps, cut 1 heart and 1 bird; reverse and cut another bird. From antique gold wool, cut 4 stars and 1 reindeer; reverse and cut another reindeer. From green wool, cut 1 tree and 1 rabbit; reverse and cut another rabbit. On right side of each animal, use white pencil to transfer markings for eyes. Pin pieces in place on wreath. Using pearl cotton, appliqué pieces to wreath using blanket stitches. Make French knots for eyes.

5. On right side of wreath, with raw edges aligned, pin scallops between dots, spreading clipped seam allowances. Baste; then machine-stitch along seam line. Set aside.

6. To prepare backing, cut remaining black wool into 2 (9½" x 18") rectangles. Referring to Diagram, with right sides facing, raw edges aligned, and backstitching at beginning and end of each seam, stitch along 1 long edge, leaving openings where indicated. Press seams open. On right side of backing unit, center and trace outer edge of wreath pattern. *Do not cut out yet.*

7. With right sides facing, align completed wreath front with marked circle on backing. Stitch completely around outer edge. Trim excess backing. Clip seam allowance and turn through center opening in backing.

8. Smooth wreath (right side up) and pin around outer edges and center. Machine-stitch center of wreath along staystitching.

Cut out center, trimming seam allowance to ⅛". Bind center opening with bias tape.

9. Stuff through openings in backing, distributing stuffing evenly. Flatten wreath and slipstitch openings closed.

For hanger loop, fold ribbon in half to form loop. Tack ends of ribbon to back of wreath at center top.

Diagram: Preparing Backing

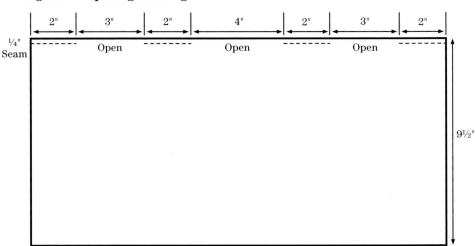

FRIENDLY NEIGHBORS ORNAMENT

Materials for one ornament

Patterns on page 143

4" x 6½" piece of maroon, antique gold, or green washed wool

5" x 15" piece of black washed wool

Polyester stuffing

Golden brown pearl cotton

White pencil

Sharp embroidery scissors

Large embroidery needle

Instructions

1. Trace selected pattern, transferring markings. Cut out.

2. From colored wool, cut 1 appliqué. Cut black wool in half widthwise to yield 2 (5" x 7½") pieces. Set 1 piece aside.

Center appliqué (right side up) on black wool (right side up) and baste in place. Using pearl cotton, appliqué in place with blanket stitches. (Make French knot for eye, if needed.)

3. Adding ½" margin around appliqué design, cut out black wool. On wrong side of cutout shape, mark ¼" seam line, using white pencil.

4. With right sides facing, center cutout shape on remaining black wool and pin in place. Machine-stitch completely around marked seam line. Trim seam; clip into crevices and curves.

Cut 1½" slit through back only. Turn through slit and stuff firmly. Flatten ornament and whipstitch opening closed.

5. To make hanger loop, thread 12½" inches of pearl cotton on embroidery needle. Take 1 stitch through ornament at center top. Remove needle and tie tails in a bow.

HOME-STYLE ACCESSORIES

◆

Use materials that are right at home in the kitchen to put together special children's accessories for Christmastime. Shop for pretty new dish towels or toweling by the yard for the apron and the small stocking. Make a cheerful, bright stocking from red-and-white tablecloth fabric or a big, super-easy stocking from a lace curtain panel.

CHILD'S ADJUSTABLE DISH TOWEL APRON

Materials
Pattern on page 146
1 hemmed dish towel, at least 18"-wide with border stripes running along long edges
8½" x 10" piece of fabric for facings
2¼ yards (½"-wide) of coordinating grosgrain ribbon or twill tape
Thread to match fabric and ribbon or tape
Large safety pin

Instructions
1. On folded paper, trace apron facing pattern, transferring markings. Cut out.

2. From fabric, cut 2 facings. Along outer curved edge of each, press under ¼" and stitch. Along each short end, press under ¾" and stitch. Set aside.

3. Referring to Diagram, Figure A, with right sides facing, align each end of 1 facing with top and side of dish towel, 5¾" from corner. Referring to pattern and backstitching at start and finish, machine-stitch ¼" from curved raw edge of facing.

Trim dish towel to match raw edge of facing seam allowance. Set aside corner scrap. Clip seam allowance. Repeat with remaining facing. Press facings to wrong side of apron and baste.

4. To make casings for neck loop and waist ties, machine-stitch open curved edge of facing to apron, backstitching at start and finish. Inside each end of each casing, slipstitch seam allowance to facing. With safety pin, thread length of ribbon or twill tape up through bottom of 1 casing and then down through top of casing on other side, leaving loop at top to go around neck. Hem each cut end of ribbon or twill tape.

5. To make decorative heart, align straight edges of 1 corner scrap; fold and press. Cut along fold. Discard the half with short stripes, as shown in Figure B. Repeat with remaining corner scrap. With right sides facing, raw edges aligned, and stripes matching, machine-stitch center seam and press open.

Referring to Figure C, using stripes as guide, and adding ¼" seam allowance, cut out heart shape. Press under seam allowance. Referring to photo, slipstitch heart to center top of apron bib.

Diagram: Making Apron

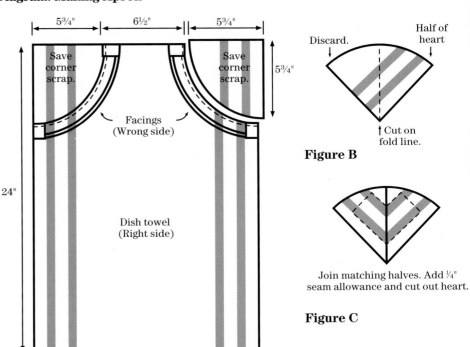

Figure A

Discard. / Half of heart

Cut on fold line.

Figure B

Join matching halves. Add ¼" seam allowance and cut out.

Figure C

Fill the Lace
Curtain Stocking (left),
Dish Towel Stocking (cen-
ter), or Tablecloth
Stocking (right) with
cookie cutters, a jar of
colored sugar, and a big
wooden spoon. Add the
Child's Adjustable Dish
Towel Apron, and you
have the perfect gift for
any young baker.

LACE CURTAIN STOCKING

Materials

Pattern on pages 146–147
¾ yard (at least 20"-wide) of curtain or valance lace
56" (¼"-wide) of matching double-fold bias tape
Thread to match
Vanishing fabric marker

Instructions

1. Trace pattern, matching dots on toe and foot sections and extending leg section of stocking 10½" as indicated on pattern.

2. On right side of lace, with border design running along top edge of stocking pattern, trace 1 stocking. Adding ¼" seam allowance, cut out. With wrong sides facing, place cut-out stocking on remaining lace, aligning border design and mesh of lace. Pin and securely baste together. Machine-stitch along side edges, leaving top open. Trim excess lace.

3. Beginning at seam at top left of stocking, slipstitch bias tape to front and back edges of stocking for binding, mitering tape at crevices. To make hanger loop, extend tape 7" beyond seam at top right. Slipstitch open edges of tape together; fold to form a loop. Turn under raw end and tack to binding on back of stocking.

TABLECLOTH STOCKING

Materials

Pattern on page 148
17" square of red-and-white check tablecloth fabric*
3 (9" x 13") pieces of red fabric for trim and lining
Thread to match
6" piece of cord for hanger
Vanishing fabric marker
*Note: See Resources, page 159.

Instructions

1. Trace pattern for stocking, adding ½" to length and transferring markings. Cut out. Trace patterns for heel A and toe; cut out.

2. On right side of tablecloth fabric, place stocking pattern so that check design is on diagonal, as shown in photo. Adding ¼" seam allowance, cut 1 front. Reverse pattern and, in same manner, cut 1 back.

3. From 1 red fabric piece, cut 2 toes and 2 heel As, adding ¼" seam allowances; then cut 2 (2⅞" x 5⅝") pieces for cuff.

4. On long straight edge of each toe and 1 long edge of each cuff piece, press under ¼". Aligning with placement lines, slipstitch pressed edges of 1 toe and 1 cuff to each stocking piece. Baste open edges to stocking. In same manner, press straight edges of heels and slipstitch in place on stocking front and back.

5. With right sides facing, center and pin stocking front to 1 piece of red lining fabric. Stitch across top edge only. Remove pins; turn and press. Baste stocking to lining; trim excess lining. Repeat with stocking back.

6. With right sides facing and raw edges aligned, pin stocking front and back together. Machine-stitch around raw edges. Carefully clip curves and into crevices. Turn stocking and press. Tack side seam allowances to front lining at top of stocking. To make hanger loop, fold cord in half. Tack ends of loop to side seam allowance at top right of stocking.

DISH TOWEL STOCKING

Materials

Pattern on page 148
18" x 24" dish towel with border stripes running along long edges
2 (9" x 13") pieces of coordinating fabric for lining
Thread to match
6" piece of cord for hanger
Vanishing fabric marker

Instructions

1. Trace pattern for stocking, adding ½" to length and transferring markings. Cut out. Trace patterns for heel B and toe; cut out.

2. On right side of dish towel, align top edge of pattern with a border stripe; adding ¼" seam allowance, cut 1 front. Reverse pattern and repeat to cut 1 back.

Referring to pattern, on remaining border scraps, trace 2 toe patterns with straight edge of each aligned with a border stripe. Adding ¼" seam allowance, cut out.

Referring to pattern, on remaining border scraps, trace 2 heel Bs with same straight edge aligned with a border stripe. Adding ¼" seam allowance, cut out. Reverse and cut 2 more.

3. On all heel Bs, press striped raw edges under ¼". With right sides facing and straight raw edges aligned, machine-stitch 2 Bs together along center seam. Press seam open. Tack excess seam allowance to back of heel unit. Repeat to make remaining heel unit. Aligning with placement lines on stocking front and back, slipstitch pressed edge of 1 heel unit to each piece. Baste open edges in place.

4. On each toe piece, press long straight edge under ¼". Aligning with placement lines, slipstitch pressed edge of 1 toe to each stocking piece. Baste open edges in place.

5. To complete, refer to Steps 5—6 of Tablecloth Stocking.

COUNTRY ACCENT

Like Christmas cards and presents, these ornaments evoke memories of secret letters to Santa and the tantalizing mysteries of brown paper packages filled with unknown goodies. They also make good use of pretty, canceled stamps saved from Christmas cards.

For the letter ornament, save small gift enclosure envelopes or make your own from plain white stationery. On the inside, align a 12" length of metallic thread along the fold of the flap. Glue the envelope closed. Knot the ends of the thread to make a hanger for your ornament. Referring to the photo, use red and green markers to add wide, diagonal strokes around the edges of the envelope. Address the letter to Santa at the North Pole and affix a canceled stamp. If you like, darken the cancellation lines with a fine-point black marker.

To make a package ornament, wrap a small jewelry box with a brown paper bag scrap. Tie the package with a bow of green string or embroidery floss. Add your own heart cutouts or tiny heart stickers to each end of the string. Address the package to a good little girl or boy and glue on a canceled Christmas stamp.

And for an extra "homespun" touch, make a quick wreath from a skein of pearl cotton. Remove the label and form the twisted skein into a ring. Slip one end of a 15" length of ribbon through each looped end of the skein and tie the ribbon in a bow. On a protected work surface, spray the wreath with heavy-duty spray starch. When this side is dry, turn the wreath over and spray the other side. Add an invisible hanger loop by tying a 10" length of monofilament to the center top.

COUNTRY CHRISTMAS TREE

◆

Surround your tree with a patchwork skirt decorated with its own forest of pine trees, a pattern popular since the mid-1800s. This design, in rich red and deep green, will add a country touch to your Christmas, whether your home is a log cabin or an apartment in the city.

Continue the country look with some quick and easy ornaments made from cardboard. You'll have great fun dabbing on the food coloring to create the "spongeware" look.

CHRISTMAS PINE TREE SKIRT

Materials
Pattern on pages 149–151
¾ yard of plain or printed muslin
⅝ yard of green print fabric
⅛ yard of brown pindot fabric
¾ yard of red print fabric
2 (28¼" x 56") pieces of muslin for backing
Thread to match
56" square of quilt batting
Vanishing fabric marker
Quilting thread (optional)
7 hook-and-eye sets

Instructions
1. Trace pattern pieces, transferring markings. Cut out.
2. Place pattern pieces on wrong side of fabrics, ½" apart. Trace and cut pieces from fabric as indicated on pattern, adding ¼" seam allowances and marking dots at all corners on seam lines.
3. Referring to Diagram 1, Figure A, assemble half of pine tree unit. In same manner, assemble reverse half of pine tree unit. Join halves to complete 1 pine tree unit (see Diagram 1, Figure B). Press all seams open. Repeat to assemble 8 complete pine tree units.

4. With right sides facing and raw edges aligned, join 2 pine tree units together along 1 long edge. Repeat in same manner to join all 8 units to form patchwork skirt, leaving 1 long edge of first and last units unstitched for opening. Along each long open edge, press under ¼" seam allowance. Set aside.

5. To make backing, with right sides facing, align long raw edges of backing pieces and pin together. Referring to Diagram 2, Figure A, machine-stitch 28" along pinned edge; backstitch. Press seam allowance open. Below stitching, press under ¼" seam allowance on each side of backing.

6. Smooth batting on flat surface and place backing (right side up) on top. Baste around outside edges and along edges of pressed seam allowances. Carefully cut batting as shown in Diagram 2, Figure B.

Turn backing unit over and whipstitch cut edge of batting to each folded seam allowance.

Turn unit to right side and smooth flat, butting together whipstitched edges along opening. With right sides facing and aligning opening between pine tree units with folded seam allowances on backing, place patchwork skirt on backing unit. Pin layers together securely along all edges, including center circle. Trim excess batting and backing.

7. Machine-stitch along outside edge and center circle. *Do not stitch along folded edges of opening.* Clip corners and into crevices. Turn right-side out. On 1 open side, slipstitch folded edges of patchwork skirt and backing together. Repeat with remaining open side.

On backing side, make small running stitches through backing, batting, and front seam allowance close to edge around center circle and outside edge. (Stitches should not go through to front.)

8. By hand or machine, stitch in-the-ditch around red borders on each patchwork unit. Stitch hook-and-eye sets at 3" intervals along opposite sides of skirt opening.

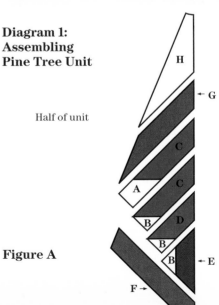

Diagram 1:
Assembling
Pine Tree Unit

Half of unit

Figure A

Diagram 2: Preparing Backing and Batting

Complete
unit
(Make 8.)

Figure B

28¼"

2 Backing pieces

28"

56"

Leave open.

Machine-stitch
to midpoint.

Figure A

Backing basted
on top of
batting layer

Right side

Cut batting
only to X.

Figure B

135

BALSAM TREE SACHET PILLOW

Materials
Pattern on page 152
7" square of plain or printed muslin
3½" x 5" piece of green print fabric
3" square of brown pindot fabric
5" square of batiste for backing
    patchwork
2 (2¾" x 5") pieces of muslin for
    pillow back
20" (¼"-wide) of brown double-fold
    bias tape
Thread to match
3 (9") pieces of brown embroidery
    floss
Balsam fir tips
Note: See Resources, page 159.

Instructions
1. Trace pattern pieces. Cut out.

2. Place pattern pieces on wrong side of fabrics, ½" apart. Trace and cut out pieces, adding ¼" seam allowances and marking dots at corners of all seams. From muslin, cut 1 U; reverse and cut 1 more; cut 6 Vs and 2 Zs. From green print, cut 4 Ws and 2 Xs. From brown pindot, cut 2 Ys.

3. Referring to Diagram, assemble 1 half of patchwork tree unit. Press all seams open. In same manner, assemble reverse half of patchwork tree unit. With right sides facing and raw edges aligned, join 2 patchwork tree units together along long straight edge. Center patchwork tree unit (right side up) on batiste and baste together. Trim excess batiste.

4. To make pillow back, with right sides facing and raw edges aligned, machine-stitch 2¾" x 5" muslin pieces together along 1 long edge, leaving 2" opening. Press seam open. With wrong sides facing, center patchwork tree unit on back and pin together. Machine-stitch together; trim back to match front.

5. Fill sachet pillow with balsam, but do not pack tightly. Slipstitch opening closed. To bind sachet pillow, slipstitch bias tape to front and back along seam line.

6. To make hanger loop, tie pieces of floss together 1" from 1 end. Tape tied end to work surface. Braid 6" length and knot ends together, forming loop. Tack knotted ends to back of pillow at center top of crevice.

Diagram:
Assembling Patchwork Tree Unit

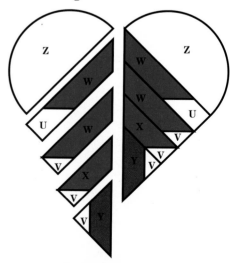

CARDBOARD "SPONGEWARE" ORNAMENTS

Materials for one ornament
Patterns on pages 152–153
Note: If making cow ornament, use
   pattern on page 72.
4½" x 6½" piece of cardboard carton
Food coloring *or* water-based paint
32" (⅛"-wide) of grosgrain ribbon to
   match
Cellulose sponge scrap
Craft knife
White glue
Ornament hanger

Instructions
   1. Trace desired pattern and cut
out.
   2. Dip sponge in undiluted food
coloring or paint. Squeeze sponge
and blot on paper towel to remove
excess; then lightly dab coloring or
paint on cardboard piece. Let dry.
Repeat on other side.
   3. From sponged cardboard, cut 1
ornament.
   4. Apply small amount of glue
along cut edge of ornament. Beginning on bottom edge, quickly glue
ribbon around ornament to cover
edge. Trim excess ribbon and cut
1¾" piece for hanger loop. While glue
is still wet, insert cut ends of ribbon
under each side of ribbon edging at
placement dots.
   For cow ornament, starting and
ending at back of cow, glue ribbon
around ornament, leaving 3" unattached for tail. To finish tail, fold cut
end of ribbon under ¾" and glue to
make a loop. Glue hanger loop under
each side of ribbon edging at center
top of cow.
   Insert ornament hanger into ribbon hanger loop.

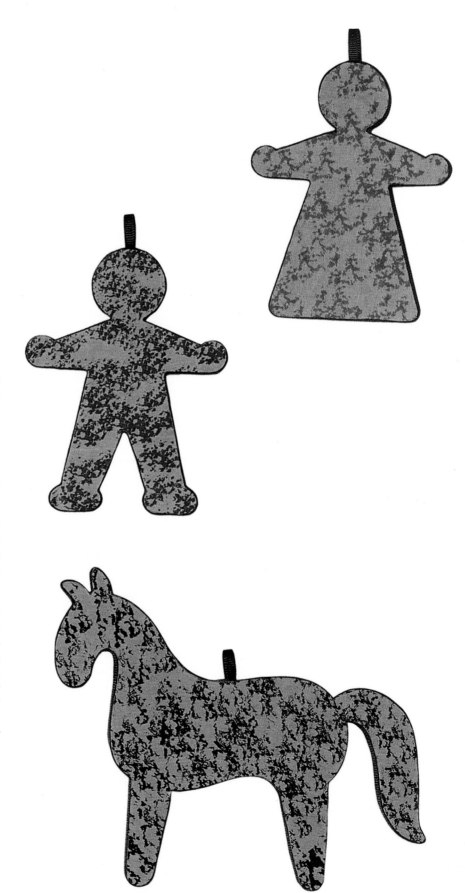

Lost Glove Bear and Sweater Bear
Instructions are on pages 116-118.

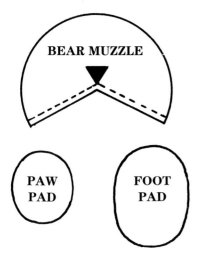

Lost Glove Baby
Instructions are on page 118.

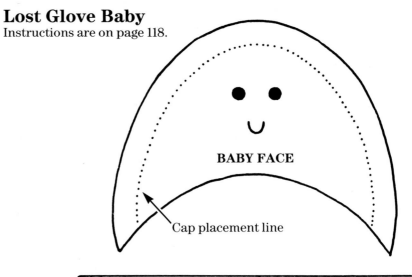

BABY FACE

Cap placement line

Snowmom and Snowbaby
Instructions are on pages 120-121.

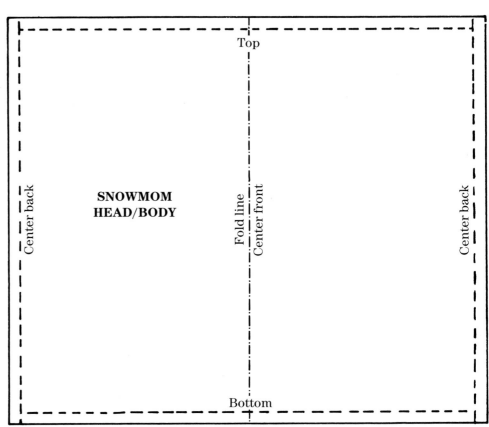

SNOWMOM ARM PIECE

Fold

Gathering line

Center front

Top

Center back

Center back

SNOWMOM HEAD/BODY

Fold line

Center front

Bottom

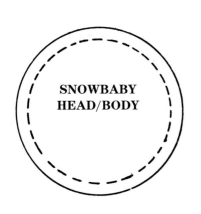

SNOWBABY HEAD/BODY

Yo-yo Santa
Instructions are on pages 122-123.

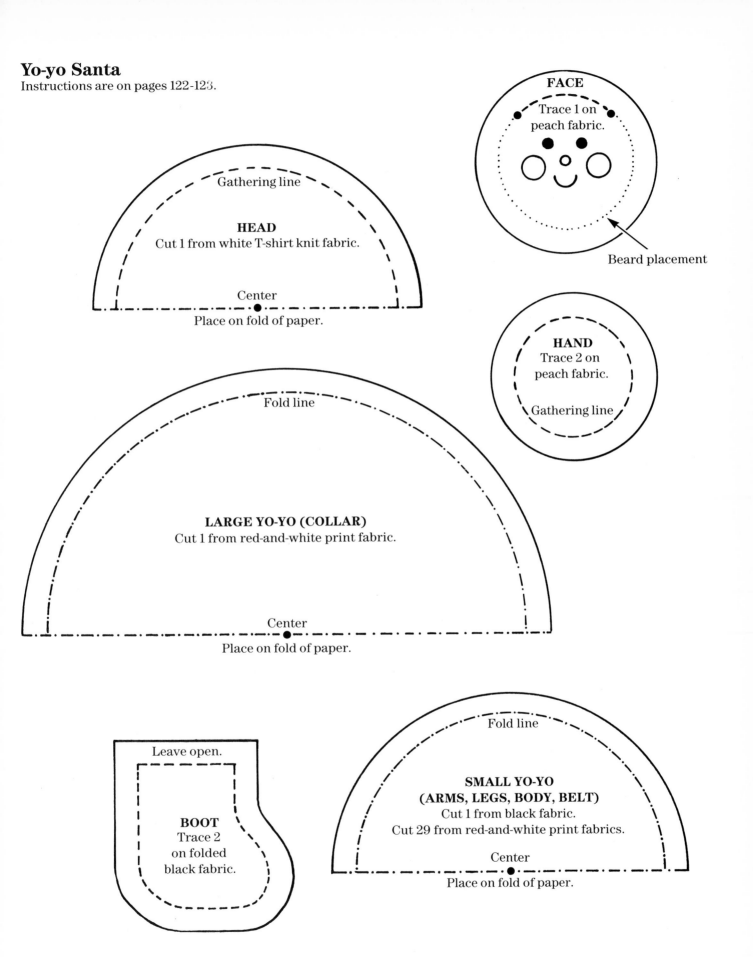

FACE
Trace 1 on peach fabric.

Beard placement

HEAD
Cut 1 from white T-shirt knit fabric.

Gathering line

Center
Place on fold of paper.

HAND
Trace 2 on peach fabric.

Gathering line

Fold line

LARGE YO-YO (COLLAR)
Cut 1 from red-and-white print fabric.

Center
Place on fold of paper.

Leave open.

BOOT
Trace 2 on folded black fabric.

Fold line

SMALL YO-YO
(ARMS, LEGS, BODY, BELT)
Cut 1 from black fabric.
Cut 29 from red-and-white print fabrics.

Center
Place on fold of paper.

Clothespin Crèche

Instructions are on page 124.

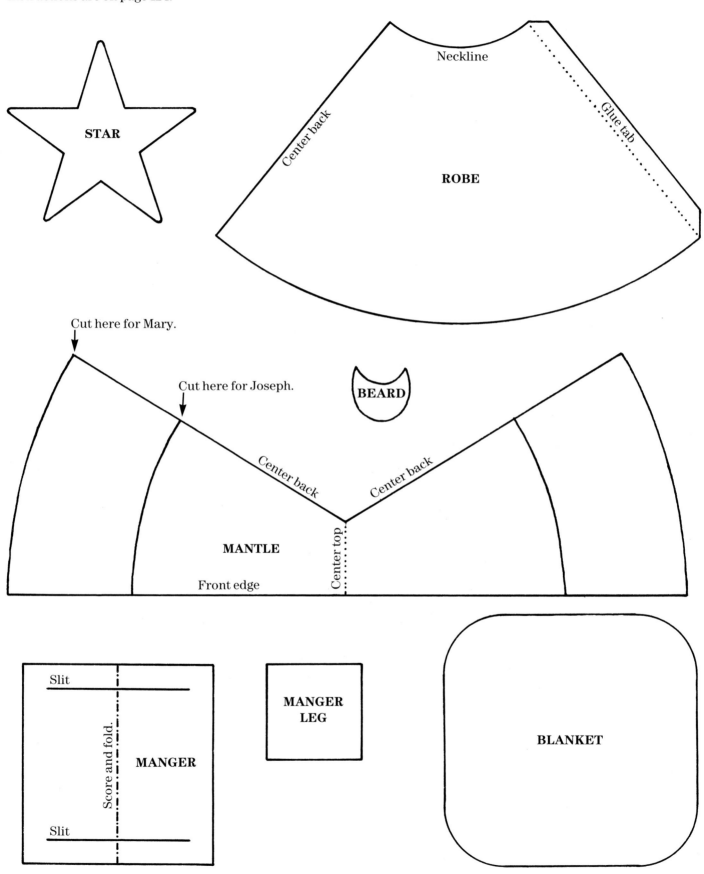

STAR

ROBE

Neckline

Center back

Glue tab

Cut here for Mary.

Cut here for Joseph.

BEARD

Center back

Center back

MANTLE

Center top

Front edge

Slit

Score and fold.

MANGER

Slit

MANGER LEG

BLANKET

Santa Clothes Ornaments

Instructions for trousers are on page 126.
Instructions for jacket are on page 127.
Instructions for boots are on page 127.

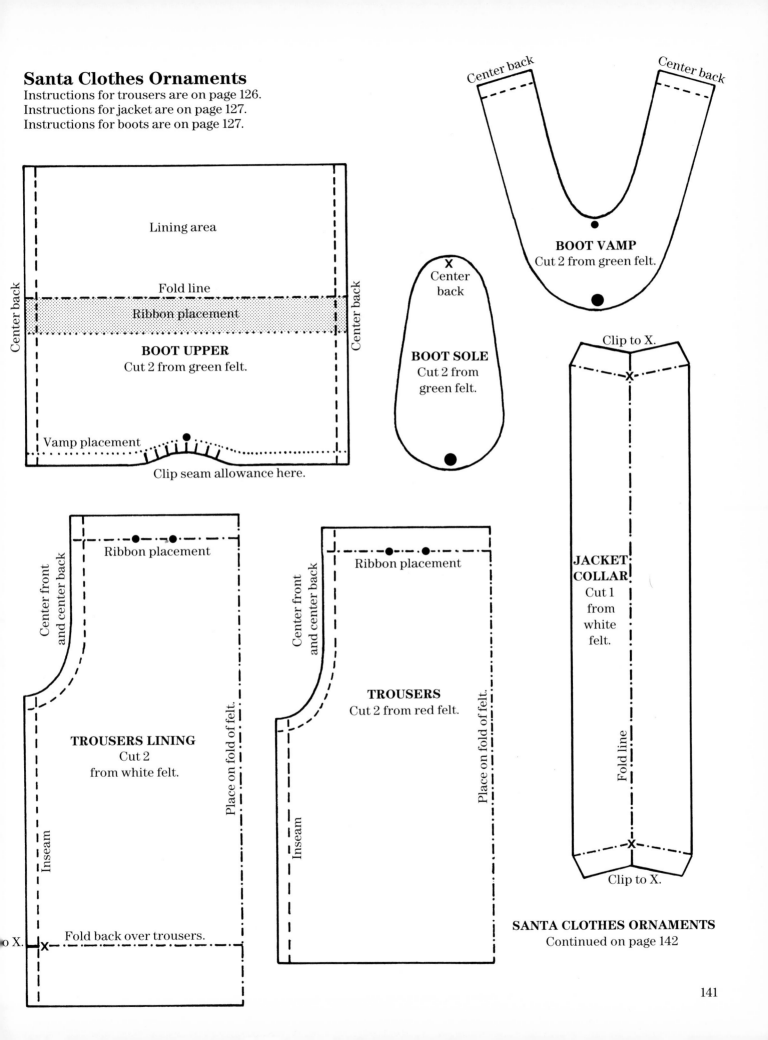

Lining area

Fold line

Ribbon placement

BOOT UPPER
Cut 2 from green felt.

Center back

Center back

Vamp placement

Clip seam allowance here.

X
Center back

BOOT SOLE
Cut 2 from green felt.

Center back

Center back

BOOT VAMP
Cut 2 from green felt.

Clip to X.

JACKET COLLAR
Cut 1 from white felt.

Fold line

Clip to X.

Center front and center back

Ribbon placement

TROUSERS LINING
Cut 2 from white felt.

Inseam

Place on fold of felt.

Fold back over trousers.

X.

X

Center front and center back

Ribbon placement

TROUSERS
Cut 2 from red felt.

Inseam

Place on fold of felt.

SANTA CLOTHES ORNAMENTS
Continued on page 142

141

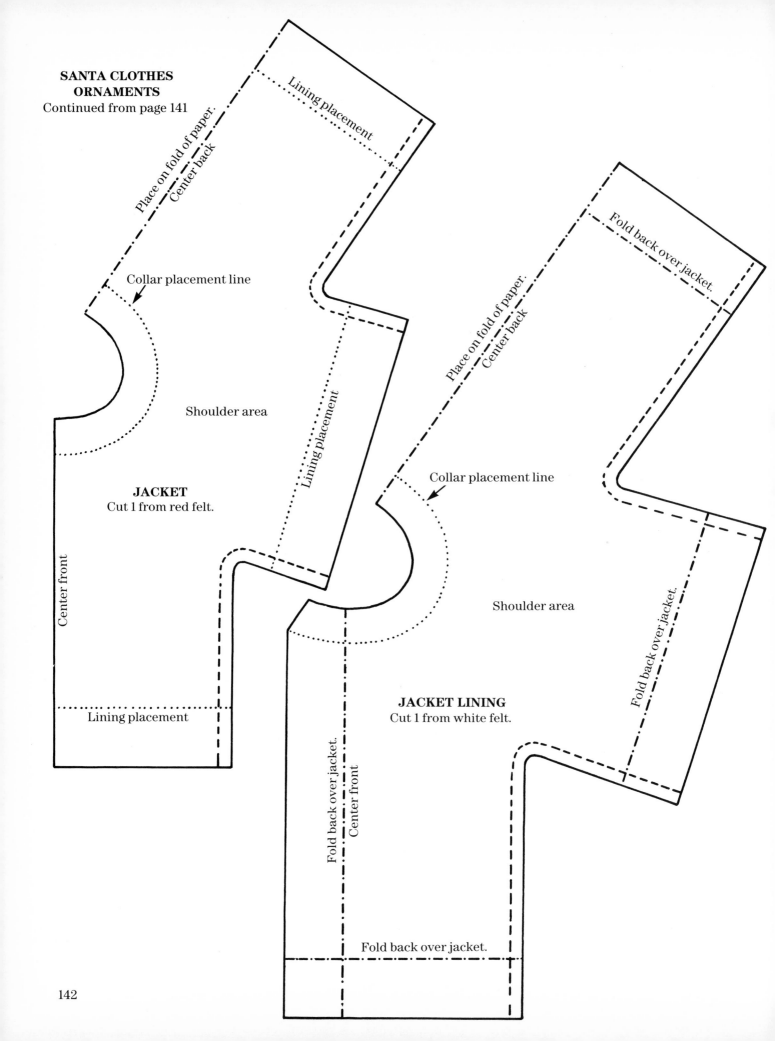

SANTA CLOTHES ORNAMENTS
Continued from page 141

Place on fold of paper.

Center back

Lining placement

Collar placement line

Shoulder area

JACKET
Cut 1 from red felt.

Lining placement

Center front

Lining placement

Collar placement line

Shoulder area

Place on fold of paper.

Center back

Fold back over jacket.

Fold back over jacket.

JACKET LINING
Cut 1 from white felt.

Fold back over jacket.

Center front

Fold back over jacket.

**Friendly Neighbors
Wreath or Ornaments**
Instructions for wreath are on page 128.
Instructions for ornaments are on page 129.

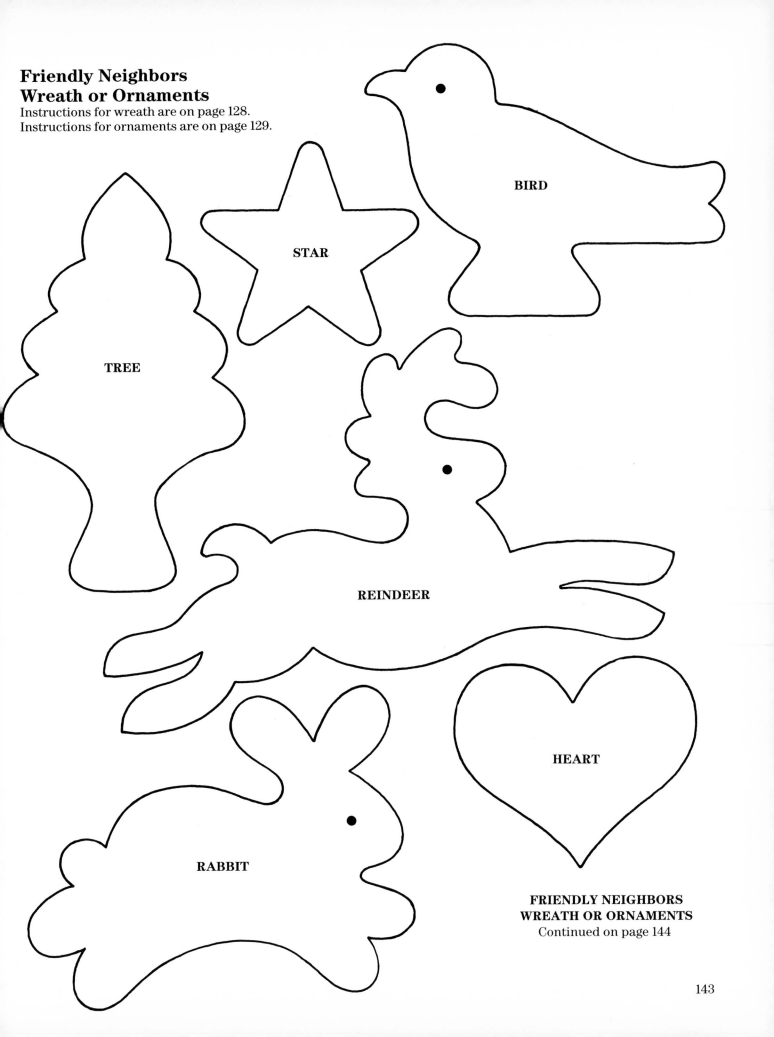

BIRD

STAR

TREE

REINDEER

HEART

RABBIT

**FRIENDLY NEIGHBORS
WREATH OR ORNAMENTS**
Continued on page 144

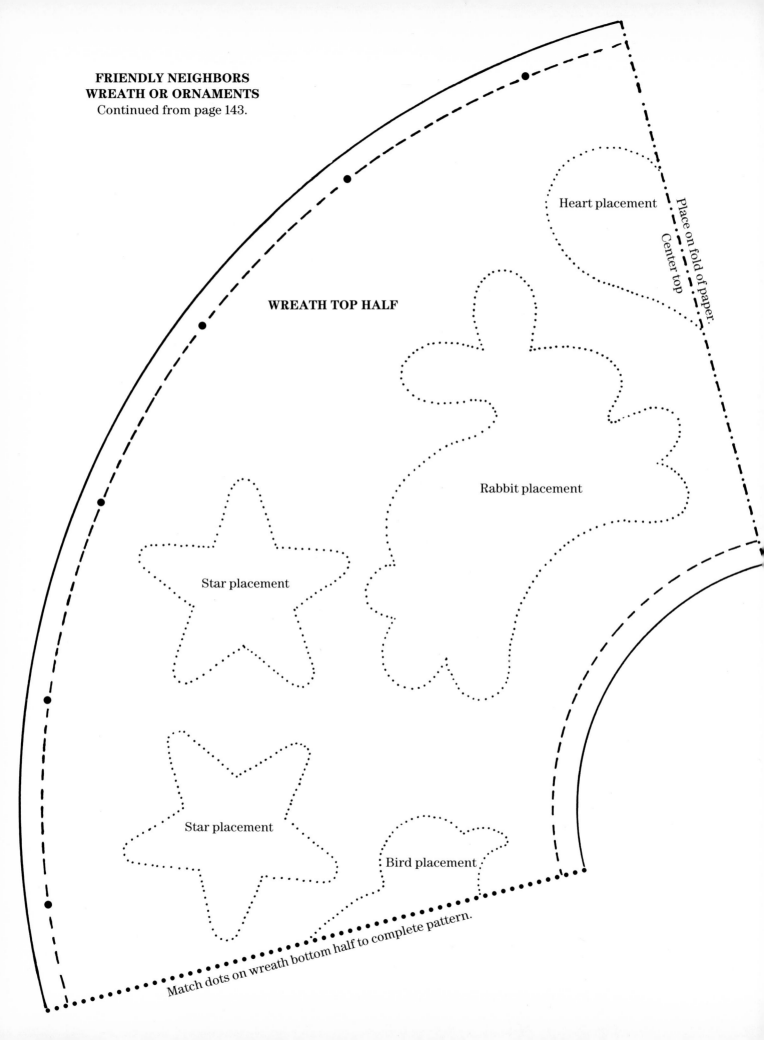

FRIENDLY NEIGHBORS
WREATH OR ORNAMENTS
Continued from page 143.

WREATH TOP HALF

Heart placement

Place on fold of paper.
Center top

Rabbit placement

Star placement

Star placement

Bird placement

Match dots on wreath bottom half to complete pattern.

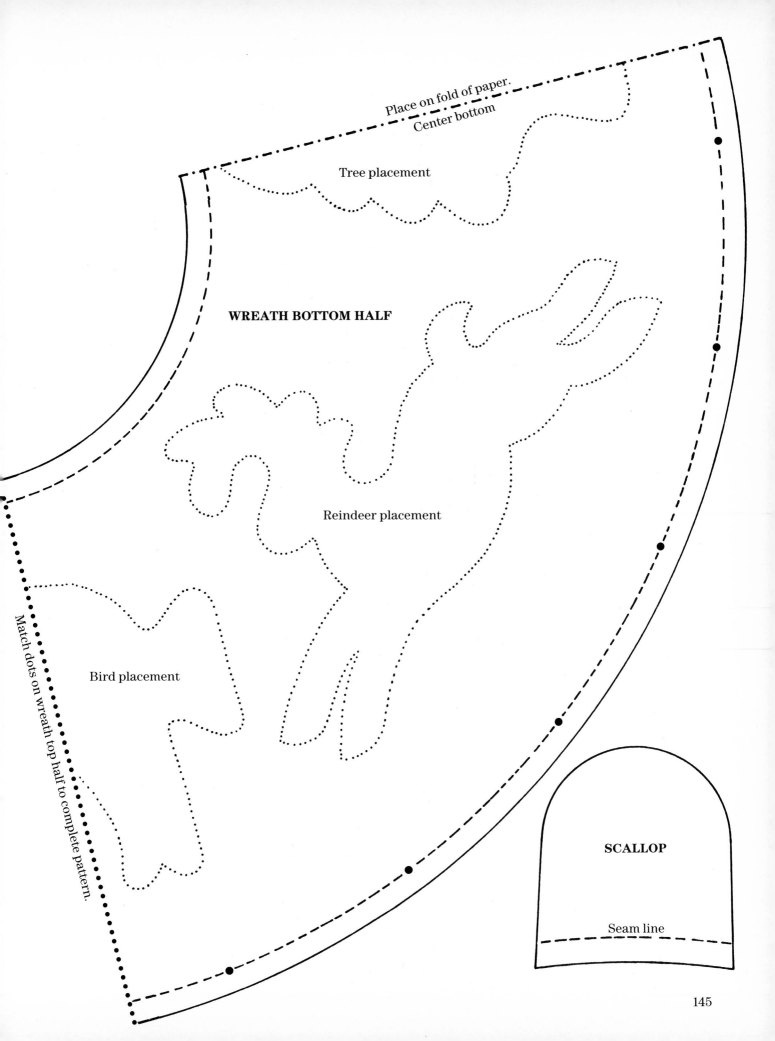

Place on fold of paper.

Center bottom

Tree placement

WREATH BOTTOM HALF

Reindeer placement

Bird placement

Match dots on wreath top half to complete pattern.

SCALLOP

Seam line

145

Lace Curtain Stocking

Instructions are on page 132.

Child's Adjustable
Dish Towel Apron

Instructions are on page 130.

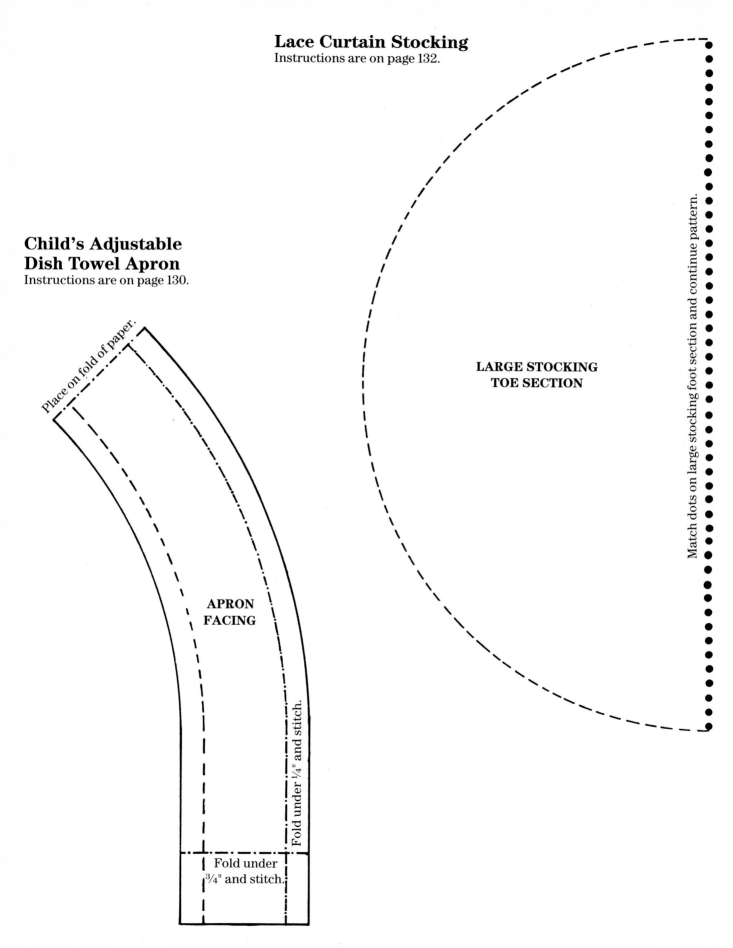

Place on fold of paper.

APRON
FACING

LARGE STOCKING
TOE SECTION

Match dots on large stocking foot section and continue pattern.

Fold under ¼" and stitch.

Fold under
¾" and stitch.

Match dots on large stocking toe section and continue pattern.

LARGE STOCKING FOOT SECTION

Extend 10½" for leg section of stocking.

147

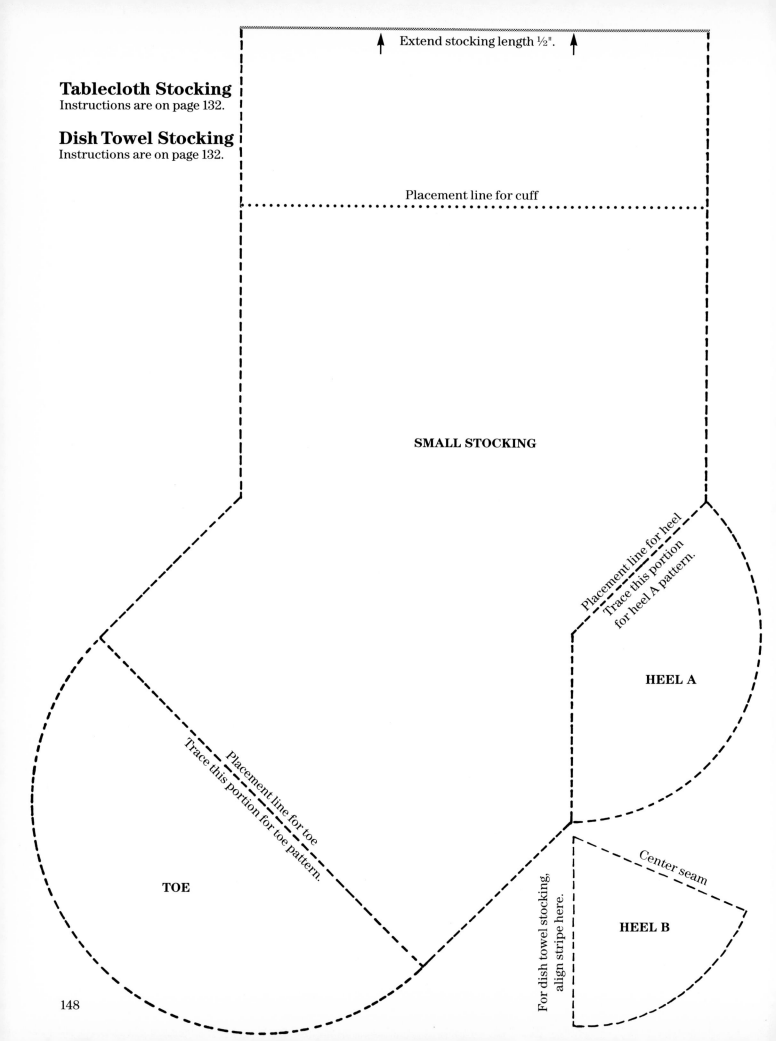

Extend stocking length ½".

Tablecloth Stocking
Instructions are on page 132.

Dish Towel Stocking
Instructions are on page 132.

Placement line for cuff

SMALL STOCKING

Placement line for heel
Trace this portion
for heel A pattern.

HEEL A

Placement line for toe
Trace this portion for toe pattern.

TOE

Center seam

For dish towel stocking, align stripe here.

HEEL B

148

Christmas Pine Tree Skirt

Instructions are on page 134.

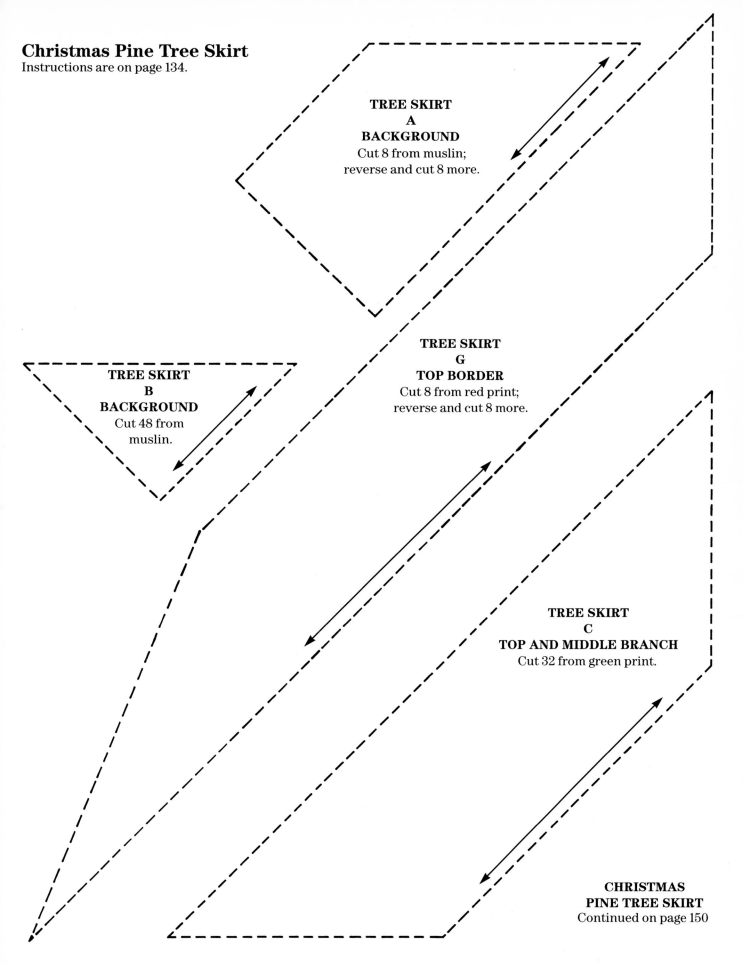

**TREE SKIRT
A
BACKGROUND**
Cut 8 from muslin;
reverse and cut 8 more.

**TREE SKIRT
B
BACKGROUND**
Cut 48 from
muslin.

**TREE SKIRT
G
TOP BORDER**
Cut 8 from red print;
reverse and cut 8 more.

**TREE SKIRT
C
TOP AND MIDDLE BRANCH**
Cut 32 from green print.

**CHRISTMAS
PINE TREE SKIRT**
Continued on page 150

149

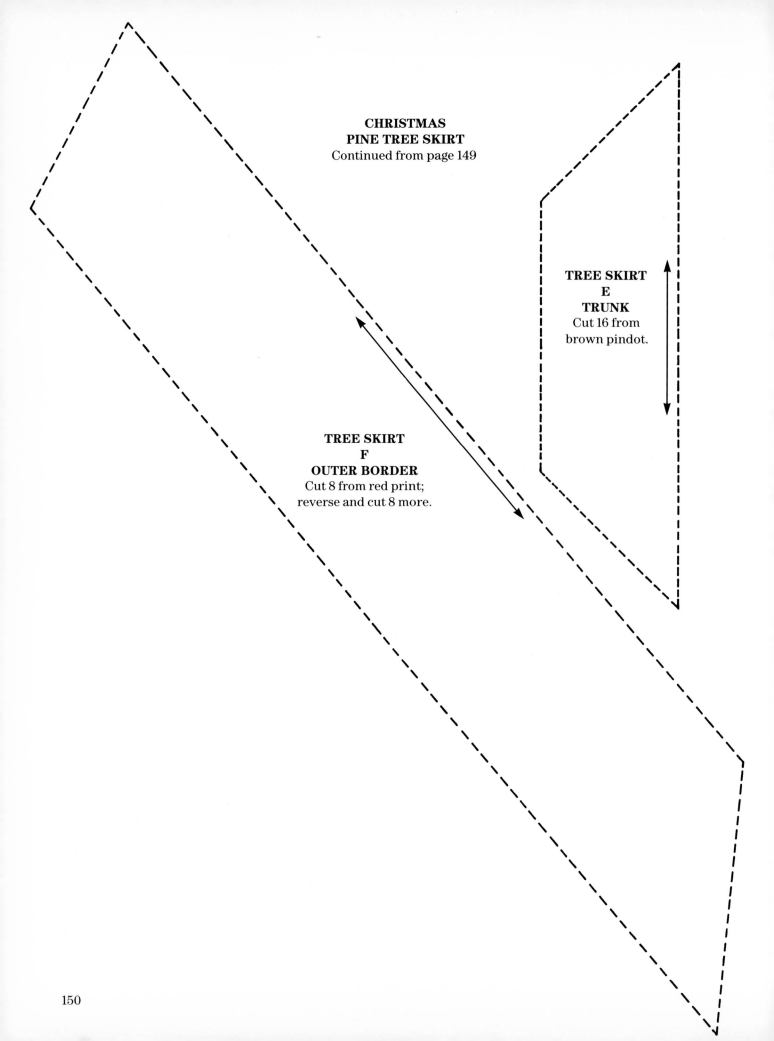

**CHRISTMAS
PINE TREE SKIRT**
Continued from page 149

**TREE SKIRT
E
TRUNK**
Cut 16 from
brown pindot.

**TREE SKIRT
F
OUTER BORDER**
Cut 8 from red print;
reverse and cut 8 more.

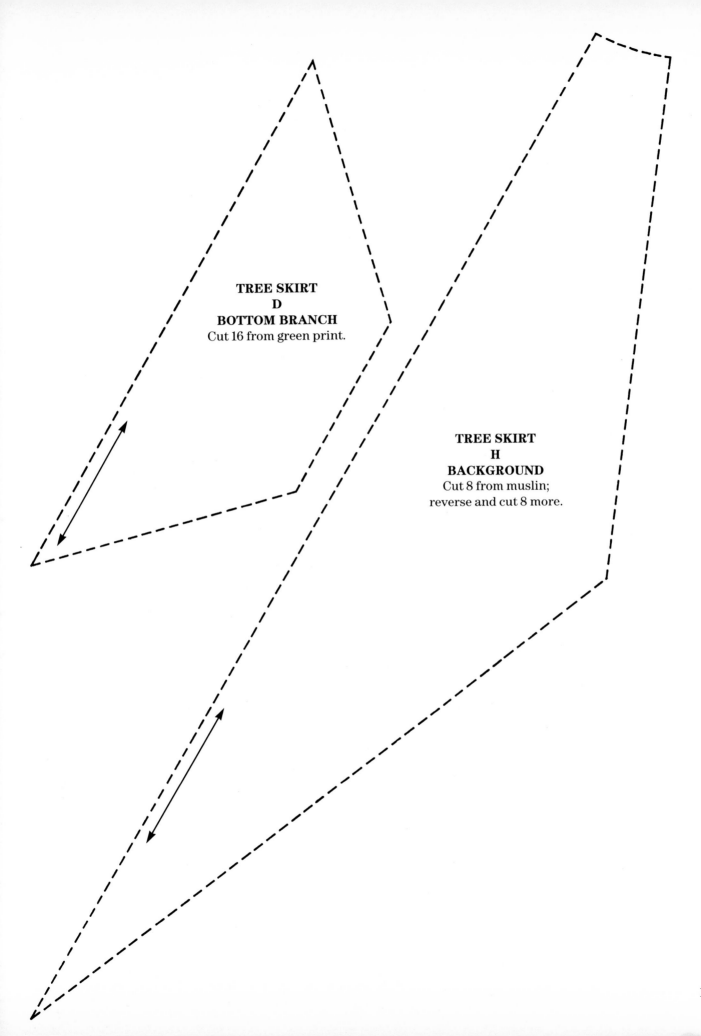

**TREE SKIRT
D
BOTTOM BRANCH**
Cut 16 from green print.

**TREE SKIRT
H
BACKGROUND**
Cut 8 from muslin;
reverse and cut 8 more.

151

Balsam Tree
Sachet Pillow
Instructions are on page 136.

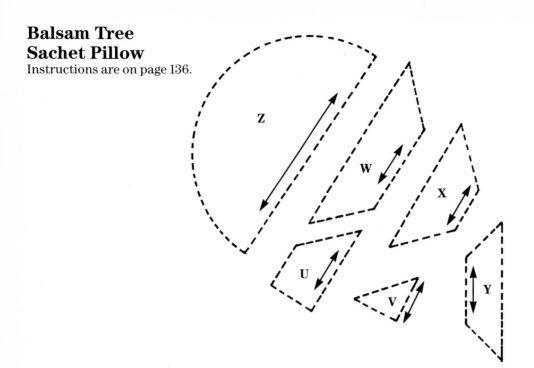

Cardboard
"Spongeware" Ornaments
Instructions are on page 137.

For **"Spongeware" Cow,**
use **Memoo Board** cow
pattern on page 72.

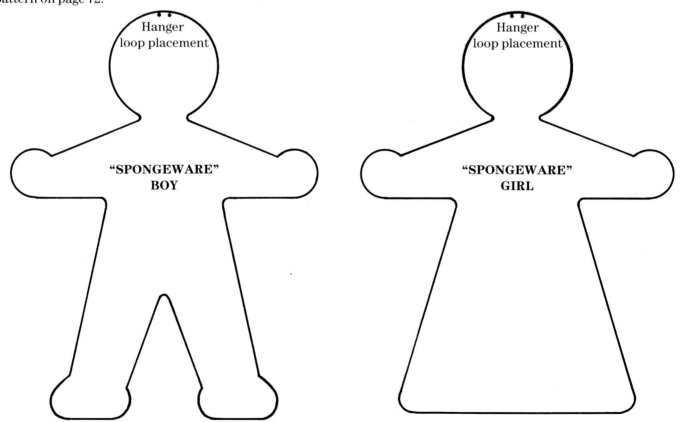

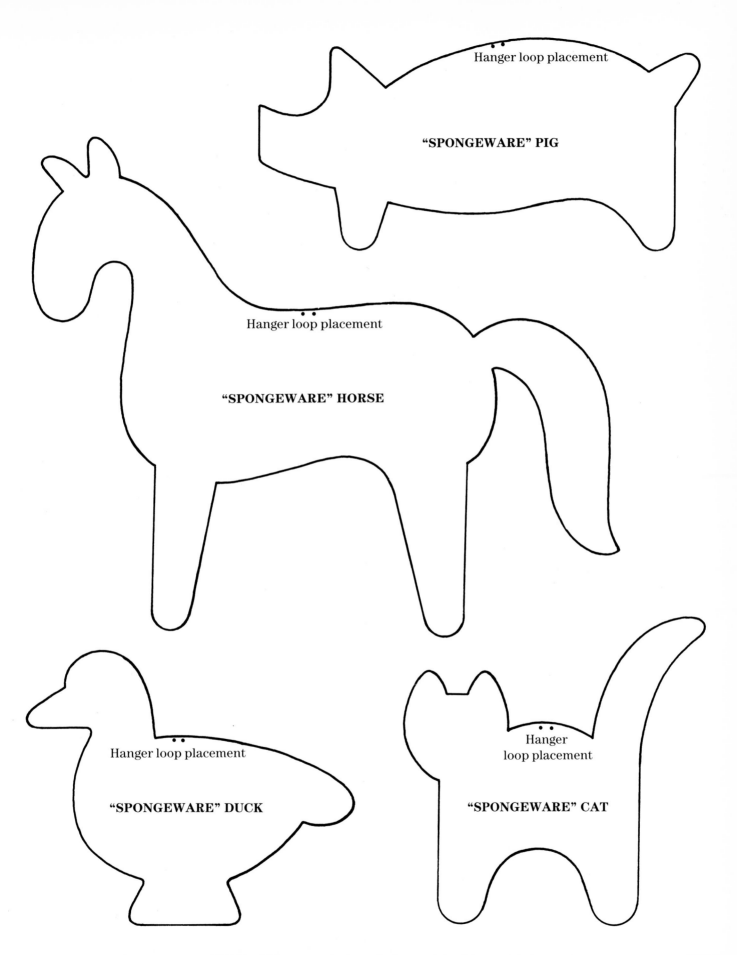

Hanger loop placement

"SPONGEWARE" PIG

Hanger loop placement

"SPONGEWARE" HORSE

Hanger loop placement

"SPONGEWARE" DUCK

Hanger
loop placement

"SPONGEWARE" CAT

153

SUPPLIES AND TECHNIQUES

◆

Take just a few moments to look over these basic steps before you get started. Then gather your own set of sewing and crafting supplies. With everything at hand, you'll be ready to cut, stitch, and make the most creative use of your time.

SEWING PROJECT SUPPLIES

Scissors. Keep your sewing scissors sharp and don't use them to cut paper. Use a 5" pair of sewing scissors for general cutting. Embroidery scissors are perfect for trimming seam allowances and cutting out little pieces. You may also wish to have a pair of 7" or 8" lightweight sewing shears for larger projects. Pinking sheers are handy for trimming seam allowances.

Rotary cutter. As an occasional alternative to scissors, a rotary cutter, used with a gridded self-healing mat and straightedge, provides a fast way to cut multiple layers of fabric.

Craft knife. I prefer an X-acto® knife with a #11 blade. I use it to make patterns, and it's especially helpful for cutting out tiny details when making a template of a pattern. Practice using this tool, keeping the hand that is not holding the knife far away from the cutting line. Work slowly and do not press down. Wrap old blades with tape before discarding.

Pattern materials. Use tracing paper to make most of the patterns. For making multiple projects, strengthen paper patterns by gluing them to thin cardboard or the

smooth side of fine sandpaper. The textured side of the sandpaper will prevent the pattern from slipping when placed on fabric.

Graph paper is great for making quick, straight-sided patterns. Purchase a pad marked with ⅛" or ¼" squares for this purpose.

Special template plastic is sold in sheets at quilt shops and at many fabric stores. Acetate is also a good material for making patterns. It can be purchased in sheets from an art supply store or saved from the tops of gift and stationery boxes. The plastic lids from coffee cans also make sturdy pattern material.

Measuring tools. I prefer a wide 15" transparent plastic sewing ruler (often referred to as "the sewer's T square") and a fabric tape measure. Both of these can be purchased at fabric stores. Instead of a yardstick for making large patterns, I use a metal ruler as a cutting edge with the craft knife. These can be purchased at art supply stores.

Drawing tools. Use sharp #2 lead pencils on light fabric and white drawing pencils on dark fabric. Mechanical pencils are a boon. Because the tip never becomes dull, they're great for tracing around patterns and transferring dots.

Use a vanishing fabric marker, available in fabric stores, when it will be necessary to remove pattern markings. It looks just like a felt-tip pen, but its ink usually fades within 48 hours and sometimes sooner. (Vanishing time varies according to the humidity. Fading takes especially long on some felt.) Always test the pen on a swatch of your fabric to make sure the ink will truly vanish.

Seam ripper. You should have a seam ripper stashed away in your workbox. And here's a hint for using it: when you need to rip dark threads from dark fabric, first highlight the stitching line with tailor's chalk.

Tweezers. They're especially handy for pulling out threads as you're ripping out seams. At times, they also help me to thread the needle of my sewing machine.

Pins and needles. Rust- and corrosion-resistant pins are less likely to snag fabrics. I love extra-long, super-strong quilting pins, but other sewers have different favorites. I prefer fine, small needles, about 1½" long, for general sewing. But you'll need large-eyed embroidery needles when using multiple strands of embroidery floss. An assortment pack of sewing machine needles is important, too, although you'll use #11 and #14 most often.

When stitching by hand through sturdy fabrics, increase the needle power by first inserting the point into a bar of soap. Wearing a few cut-off fingers from an old rubber glove will help you pull the needle through thick batting.

Pin keepers. Although magnetic pin dispensers are a bit expensive, they're convenient and spill-proof, and they're also helpful to locate stray pins. I use several pincushions or dispensers at once, placing one at the cutting area, one at the sewing machine, and one at the ironing board. Another neat pin keeper is an adhesive-backed magnetic strip that attaches to the flat surface of your sewing machine and attracts pins that wander too close to the needle or bobbin area.

Quilt batting. In most cases, use traditional-weight polyester batting. When necessary, however, you can substitute several thin layers for one thick layer. Purchase a crib-quilt-size piece for small projects and save the scraps for stuffing toys and pillows. If the batting is sold in a fat sausage shape, remove it from the plastic bag and unroll it at least a day before you plan to use it, allowing it to relax and let the wrinkles smooth out. A short tumble in a warm dryer will also help to diminish wrinkles.

Pressing equipment. Pressing is very important for successful sewing, so place your ironing board near the sewing machine, if possible. Be sure to keep the iron's sole plate clean. Check it often, especially after using fusible web.

A pressing cloth is a necessity, even if it's just a good-sized scrap of lightweight fabric. A small tailor's ham isn't a necessity, but it's helpful when pressing curved seams.

Other helpful tools. There are a few more tools that will help you. Embroidery hoops are useful when doing decorative hand stitchery. A 3"- or 4"-diameter hoop is handy for small projects, and an 8"-diameter hoop is also used.

For turning and stuffing small pieces, try a crochet hook or a pencil with a blunted point (no lead showing). For larger work, use a wooden yardstick or a dowel. Once shapes are turned right side out, use a long sturdy needle to pull out corners and curves, but take care to avoid snagging the fabric.

Washable fabric glue is a great time-saver, and the thicker its consistency, the less it will soak through the fabric. Always apply the glue sparingly. A glue stick is useful for quick basting jobs. Always test the glue on a fabric swatch before applying it to a final project. Allow the glue to dry thoroughly before you proceed with sewing.

Masking tape is a sewer's friend. When tracing patterns from a book, use it to anchor the tracing paper. (When you've finished tracing, the tape lifts off easily.) Masking tape can also be placed on the throat plate of your sewing machine to mark the seam allowance width. When you are machine stitching a project that has a top layer of batting, the presser foot often catches the top fibers. To avoid this nuisance, wrap the "toes" of the presser foot together with a single piece of tape.

Applying liquid ravel preventer to all cut ends of ribbons will prevent fraying.

Fabrics. When yardages are given, it should be assumed that the fabrics are at least 44" wide, unless otherwise specified. Lay out all the pattern pieces as close to each other as possible, but maintain enough space for seam allowances, if they need to be added.

Inspect fabrics carefully before you buy them and avoid those that fray easily. Use light- to medium-weight fabrics, unless others are suggested, and prewash them.

When the grain of the fabric is important to the design, grain lines are marked on the patterns, and you should lay out patterns accordingly. Since felt isn't woven, it doesn't have a grain, so you can place patterns freely. Because the iron heat and moisture can cause felt to shrink, steam away wrinkles before cutting felt. Most felt is not washable, but there is some beautiful washable felt available now. For this felt, I recommend gentle hand washing and line drying.

SEWING PROJECT TECHNIQUES

Making patterns. Draw neat and accurate patterns, copying all the matching dots, embroidery and placement lines, and labeling each piece. Or, to copy patterns quickly, use a photocopier. Though all the patterns in this book are protected by copyright, you may photocopy them to make these projects for your personal use.

Because of space limitations, frequently only one half of a pattern has been drawn in this book. To make a complete pattern, trace these half patterns on folded tracing paper, transferring markings to both right and left sides. Half patterns in this book are not meant to be placed on folded fabric unless the instructions state otherwise.

Before you trace the patterns, read the directions for each project and determine whether the seam allowances are included or must be added. *Unless otherwise noted in the instructions, all seam allowances for these projects will be ¼".*

Solid pattern lines indicate cutting lines for fabrics and felt, broken lines indicate stitching lines, fine dotted lines indicate placement lines, and alternating broken and dotted lines indicate fold lines.

I frequently cut quilt patterns from acetate and then, using nail polish, I label them and paint a thin layer of color around the edges. This outlining makes it easier to center the transparent patterns on the fabric motifs. It also helps me to locate the patterns quickly. Because of the painted label, I can also tell at a glance when the pattern is reversed.

Marking fabrics. Unless otherwise instructed, place the pattern face down on the wrong side of the fabric, hold or pin it in place, and draw around it with a sharp pencil.

When drawing small pattern pieces on fabrics, first place an 8½" x 11" piece of fine-textured sandpaper on your work surface. With this base, the fabric will not be pulled as much when you draw around the patterns.

Transferring markings. There are several ways to transfer embroidery or placement lines to the right side of the fabric:

1. You can make a stencil of some patterns, such as those for facial features, by cutting out the details. Center the pattern on the front of the cutout fabric shape and draw the details, using very light pencil strokes or a vanishing fabric marker. Or draw the details on the back of the fabric and transfer them to the front with tiny basting stitches.

2. To transfer details using the rub-off technique, go over the details on the back of the patterns with a sharp #2 lead pencil. Center the pattern on the front of the fabric piece and then rub off the design with a flat wooden stick or a similar burnisher. This can get a little messy.

3. A sunny window can also be used to transfer pattern details. Tape the pattern to the wrong side of a piece of fabric of manageable size and trace the pattern outline. Then tape the fabric and pattern to the window (pattern against the glass) and lightly trace the details onto the right side of the fabric.

4. When transferring details to felt, use the following method: Instead of making a template of the pattern, use a large needle to make holes along the pattern lines. Hold the pattern against the felt shape and carefully mark through the holes with a sharp pencil.

5. When I embroider facial details on a stuffed toy, I often draw the features with a vanishing fabric marker after the head is stuffed. Since filling can distort the face considerably, I wait until after the head is formed to find the best position for the face.

Whichever method you use, draw lightly. Once you've marked the right side of the fabric, do not iron over the drawing, because the heat may set the lines permanently, even those made with a vanishing marker.

Stitching and trimming seams. Although shortcuts are tempting, it's really best to pin and baste your fabric pieces together before stitching them. If there are dots to be matched, line up the pieces, right sides together, and push a pin straight down through both fabric layers at the dots. Then pin along the seam allowance (but not on the seam line) perpendicular to the edge. Baste, remove pins, and then machine-stitch the seams.

I don't advise sewing over pins. There's too much chance of injuring your machine or yourself!

Grading seam allowances. To make seams smooth on the right side, bulky seam allowances (those involving several layers of fabric or batting) should be graded. Cut each layer of the seam allowance a different distance from the stitching line. For instance, if a seam allowance is ½" wide, trim the bottom layer to ⅜" and the top layer to ¼". Always cut across corners, trimming close to the stitching. Make vertical clips in the seam allowance on curves, clipping almost to the stitching line.

Gathering. When making long machine stitches that will be gathered, two closely placed rows of stitches, ⅛" apart, are better than one. If you use different colors for the top and bobbin threads, it will be easy to identify the bobbin thread to pull for gathering.

Applying bias tape. Before binding an edge with bias tape, trim the seam allowance so that it is about 1/16" narrower than the bias tape. If the seam allowances are very thick, zigzag-stitch edges to flatten. Clip into any angles around the shape.

When using double-fold bias tape or quilt binding as a flat trim, use the following method: Open the center fold of the tape and trim one folded edge ⅛" or more from the center fold. Discard the trimming.

Mitering bias tape. Refer to the illustrations and the instructions in Diagram.

Quilting. When batting is sandwiched between two pieces of fabric, the layers must be pinned and basted together so that they won't shift. Work from the center to the outside of the piece, making 1" stitches horizontally, vertically, and diagonally across the piece. To quilt, use a short quilting needle and make uniform running stitches through all layers. Gather several stitches on your needle before pulling the thread through the fabric. Quilting stitches are usually placed ¼" from the seam line, but I sometimes quilt right on the seam line or "in-the-ditch." For machine quilting, use long straight stitches.

Adding appliqué. If you plan to handstitch an appliqué, the piece must be cut with a hem allowance. For the best results, make tiny basting stitches along the outline of the appliqué shape to create a precise folding edge for the hem. To make the hemming of small pieces easier, cut them out with pinking shears or clip hem allowances at close intervals. Turn under the hem allowance and baste. Pin and baste the shape in place and appliqué it invisibly with slipstitches, or blanket-stitch the edge of the shape.

If you intend to attach an appliqué with machine zigzag stitches, it need not be cut with a hem allowance. To secure the appliqué before stitching, use fusible web to attach it to the fabric and then stitch with very close zigzag stitches.

Stuffing and such. Polyester stuffing is easiest to work with. Keep it clean and free of thread and fabric clippings.

It's best to add stuffing in small quantities. When filling a doll or an animal, start with the smaller parts, such as the arms, legs, and head. Really pack in the stuffing, with the aid of a crochet hook, blunt pencil, or a wooden spoon handle. Have an extra bag of stuffing on hand. You'll almost always need more than you expect. (Most projects need to be firmly stuffed, although occasionally a project will require a flat, softly stuffed appearance.) Mold the item with your hands as you stuff it.

Some words of caution. Please don't add buttons, bells, pom-poms, or similar embellishments to gifts that will go to households with very young children. Heed my advice if I suggest that a certain design is not intended to be a plaything. There are lots of gifts for little ones in this book, so choose the safe ones and stitch them securely, using pre-washed materials.

Diagram: Mitering Bias Tape Used as a Binding

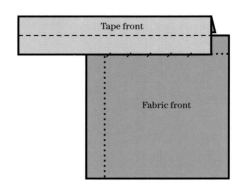

Figure A: Open center fold of tape and place one edge of tape along placement line. Slipstitch tape to the front of the fabric.

Figure B: At the corner, fold the loose end of the tape toward wrong side of the fabric at a 45-degree angle.

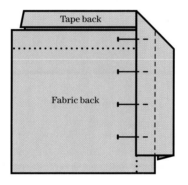

Figure C: Turn the work over and pin the tape along placement line as shown.

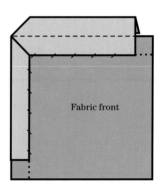

Figure D: Turn the work to the right side. Fold the flap of pinned tape toward the right side and slipstitch to the fabric.

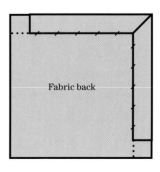

Figure E: Turn the work to the wrong side, fold down the remaining tape, and pin in position. Slipstitch the tape to wrong side of fabric.

157

PAPER PROJECT SUPPLIES

Paper. To assure best results, use sturdy, high-quality paper such as Canson or Crescent when making the paper projects in this book. These richly hued papers can be found in art supply stores. Or consider colored paper used for pastel drawings and watercolors. Some large photocopy stores offer beautifully colored heavyweight paper for sale by the sheet. Don't be tempted to substitute construction paper. It often splits when scored and folded.

Cutting tools. You'll need a cutting board or a piece of heavy cardboard (not corrugated) to protect your work surface. I prefer an X-acto® knife with a new #11 blade for cutting and scoring. Keep an extra supply of blades on hand. Dull blades make ragged, inaccurate cuts. Standard ¼" and ⅛" paper punches are frequently used for paper projects in this book.

PAPER PROJECT TECHNIQUES

Making patterns. Accuracy is essential when drawing and cutting patterns for paper projects. A photocopier is the most efficient way to copy paper project patterns. Photocopy the pattern directly from the book, glue the photocopy to lightweight cardboard or plastic if you wish, and cut out the pattern.

If no photocopier is available, trace the pattern and markings onto tracing paper, glue the tracing paper to cardboard or plastic, and cut out the pattern on the outline.

Marking paper. Transfer patterns to art paper with a very sharp #2 lead pencil. Score the folds by lightly drawing the craft knife blade over the fold line.

Other hints. To increase the art paper's flexibility on pieces that will be curved, such as bows and basket handles, gently pull the piece over a table edge or scissors blade. The paper will curl slightly, making it easier to bend into shape.

To keep your hands free for other tasks, hold the glued areas of paper projects together for drying with paper clips or clip clothespins.

EMBROIDERY STITCHES

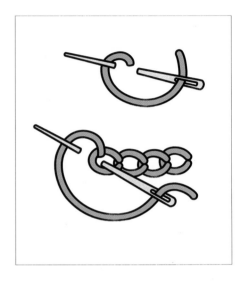

Chain stitch. Working from right to left, or top to bottom, depending on your preference, bring the needle up and make a loop with the thread. Holding the loop against the fabric, insert the needle again, as close as possible to where the thread last emerged. Take a short stitch over the looped thread to anchor it.

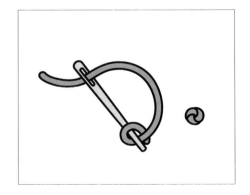

French knot. Bring the needle up where you want an embroidered dot. Wrap the thread several times around the point of the needle. Insert the needle again as close as possible to the spot where the thread emerged. Holding the wraps in place, pull the thread to the wrong side.

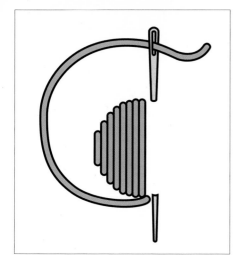

Satin stitch. Working from one end of a figure to the other, bring the needle up on one side and insert it on the opposite side. Carrying the thread behind the work, repeat from side to side, keeping the stitches parallel, smooth, and close together.

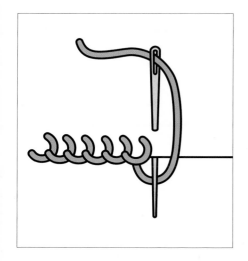

Blanket stitch. This is a stitch for edge finishing. Bring the needle out along the edge of the fabric. Insert the needle above and to the right of the starting point and bring it out in line with the last stitch on the fabric edge, keeping the thread behind the needle point. Continue working from left to right and top to bottom.

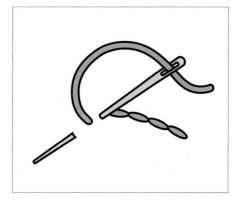

Backstitch. Working from right to left, or top to bottom, bring the needle up on the guideline. Take a stitch backward and bring the needle up an equal distance ahead of the first hole made by thread. Repeat, taking the needle back to the end of the previous stitch.

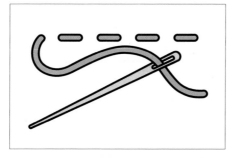

Running stitch. Working from right to left, make stitches of the same size, with even spaces between them. Use running stitches for quilting, gathering several stitches on the needle before pulling the thread through the fabric.

RESOURCES

◆

Y ou'll find most of the supplies and materials for the projects in this book at your local stores. If these items are not available in your area, please write to the following companies to receive catalog information:

Cookie Cutters
Maid of Scandinavia
3244 Raleigh Avenue
Minneapolis, MN 55416

Red-and-White Tablecloth Fabric
Vermont Country Store
Mail Order Office
P.O. Box 3000
Manchester Center, VT 05255-3000

Lavender and Potpourri
The Rosemary House
120 South Market Street
Mechanicsburg, PA 17055

Balsam Fir Tips
Maine Balsam
P.O. Box 9
West Paris, ME 04289
(Please enclose a self-addressed, stamped envelope.)

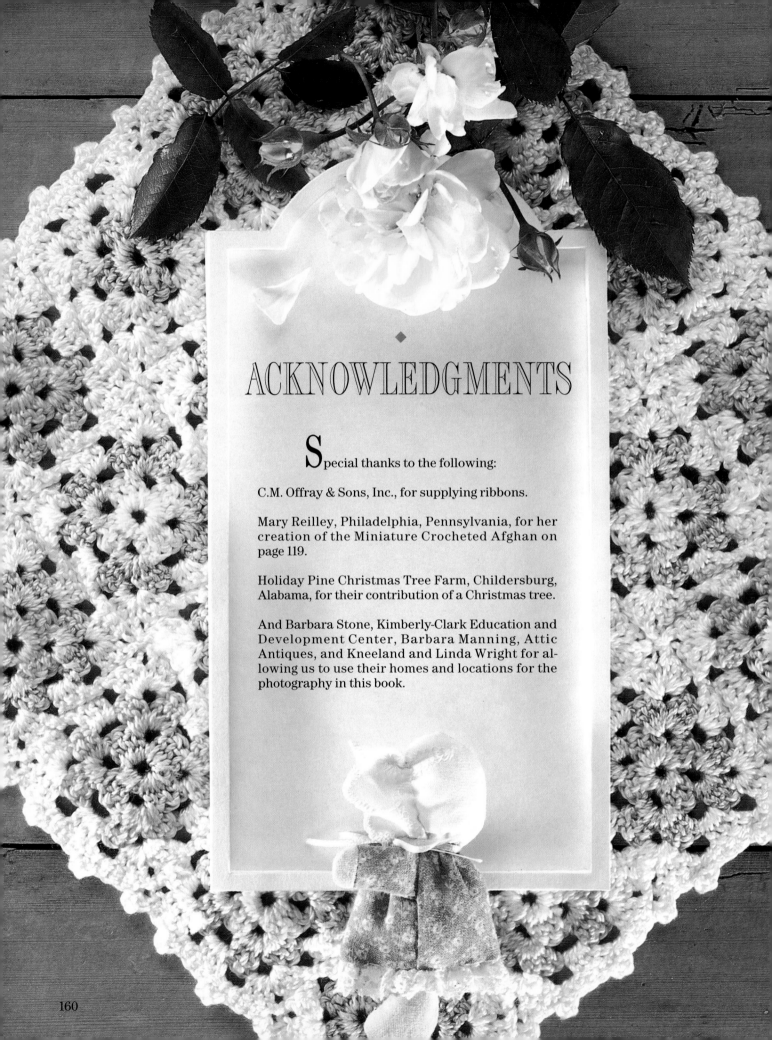

ACKNOWLEDGMENTS

Special thanks to the following:

C.M. Offray & Sons, Inc., for supplying ribbons.

Mary Reilley, Philadelphia, Pennsylvania, for her creation of the Miniature Crocheted Afghan on page 119.

Holiday Pine Christmas Tree Farm, Childersburg, Alabama, for their contribution of a Christmas tree.

And Barbara Stone, Kimberly-Clark Education and Development Center, Barbara Manning, Attic Antiques, and Kneeland and Linda Wright for allowing us to use their homes and locations for the photography in this book.